R

Promotion for Sport Directors

John R. Johnson
Michigan High School Athletic Association

Human Kinetics

y of Congress Cataloging-in-Publication Data

Johnson, John R., 1955–
Promotion for sportdirectors / John R. Johnson.
p. cm.
Includes index.
ISBN 0-87322-722-0 (paper)
1. Public relations--United States--Sports. 2. Sports administration--United States. I. Title.
GV714.J64 1996
659.2'9'7960973--dc20 95-34843
CIP

ISBN: 0-87322-722-0

Acquisitions Editor: Jim Kestner; **Developmental Editor:** Jan Colarusso Seeley; **Assistant Editors:** Erin Cler and Kirby Mittelmeier; **Copyeditor:** Jim Kestner; **Proofreader:** Sue Fetters; **Indexer:** Barbara E. Cohen; **Typesetter and Layout Artist:** Francine Hamerski; **Text and Cover Designer:** Stuart Cartwright; **Photographer (interior):** John R. Johnson; **Illustrators:** Patrick Griffin, cartoons; and Stuart Cartwright; **Printer:** Versa Press

Printed in the United States of America 10 9 8 7 6 5 4 3 2 1

Human Kinetics
P.O. Box 5076, Champaign, IL 61825-5076
1-800-747-4457

Canada: Human Kinetics, Box 24040,
Windsor, ON N8Y 4Y9
1-800-465-7301 (in Canada only)

Europe: Human Kinetics, P.O. Box IW14,
Leeds LS16 6TR, United Kingdom
(44) 1132 781708

Australia: Human Kinetics, 2 Ingrid Street,
Clapham 5062, South Australia
(08) 371 3755

New Zealand: Human Kinetics,
P.O. Box 105-231, Auckland 1
(09) 523 3462

To Suzie, who helps me understand these are kids' games, not life and death situations.

To Nick, who taught me to treat the media evenhandedly at all times.

To Jack, one of my best mentors ever.

To my Lord, Jesus Christ. Without Him, none of this is possible.

Contents

Foreword

Changes in American society during the past century have made it increasingly difficult to attract a live audience to an event. Just think about the changes and some of their unpredictable outcomes. The automobile made us more mobile to travel to whatever we choose to enjoy. More and more enjoyments developed, dividing our attention ever more. Radio begat television. No longer was it something remarkable to listen to an athletic event on the radio with some great wordsmith crafting visual pictures in our minds. Television started dominating our lives, and satellites magnified the ability to deliver a sporting program directly into our living rooms. At every level various sports scrambled to be *the* provider of entertainment to a sporting world, from professional sports to made-for-television events, from college events to the high school state championships. The entertainment dollar was divided up even more.

Still, the cornerstone of a person's athletic interest and loyalty is the hometown high school with its interscholastic athletic program. No greater rallying point for a community exists than the ol' hometown high. People wish to enjoy just one more time their memories of games gone by, being recreated now by the newest generation of high school athletes, both male and female. Conducting home interscholastic athletic programs has become a major endeavor for administrators and coaches. I know what it takes, in terms of personnel and resources, for a program the size of Indiana University's to conduct a home football or mens basketball game, so I have to marvel at the high school or junior high school administrator attempting to do the same things in a local community with only a fraction of the staff and dollars that we can call on. That local administrator may have been thrust into the game management role without any background or knowledge of what it takes. Where should that person turn to find out how to attract and retain the local audience to support hometown high? How do you raise enough funds to keep all the sports going, let alone think about adding sports to create equity between men's and women's programs?

Promotion for SportDirectors is a tremendous resource that provides excellent practical examples and tips of what to do and how to do it. I've known John Johnson for well over 10 years, and he is one of the most innovative communicators, bar none, in intercollegiate or interscholastic athletics today. He's been a visionary with ideas and ways to communicate about and to promote events. This book is a veritable road map for how you can be successful in your situation. From what I've read in *Promotion for SportDirectors*, I've learned a thing or two that's going to come in handy working with the Indiana University home event management. But then, that's the influence and impact John Johnson has always had on me. He's done a great service to athletics by taking the time to pen his thoughts and ideas in *Promotion for SportDirectors*.

Charles K. Crabb
Associate Athletic Director for
Events and Facilities
Indiana University

Series Preface

The SportDirector Series is a revolutionary approach to the craft of managing athletic programs. Underlying the resources in this series is a set of principles drawn from a careful examination of the day-to-day responsibilities sport directors face. These principles have been framed as a sequence of tests, which each series resource has been designed to pass:

- Is the resource practical?
- Is it affordable?
- Does it save time?
- Is it easy to use?
- Is it up-to-date?
- Is it flexible enough to meet the needs of different programs?
- Does using one resource from the series make it easier to use others?

To ensure that every resource passes these tests, we have worked closely with an editorial advisory board of prominent, experienced athletic directors from across the nation. With the board's assistance, we have developed the series to enable you to benefit from the latest thinking in directing sport programs. Each resource leads you carefully through three steps: planning, implementing, and evaluating.

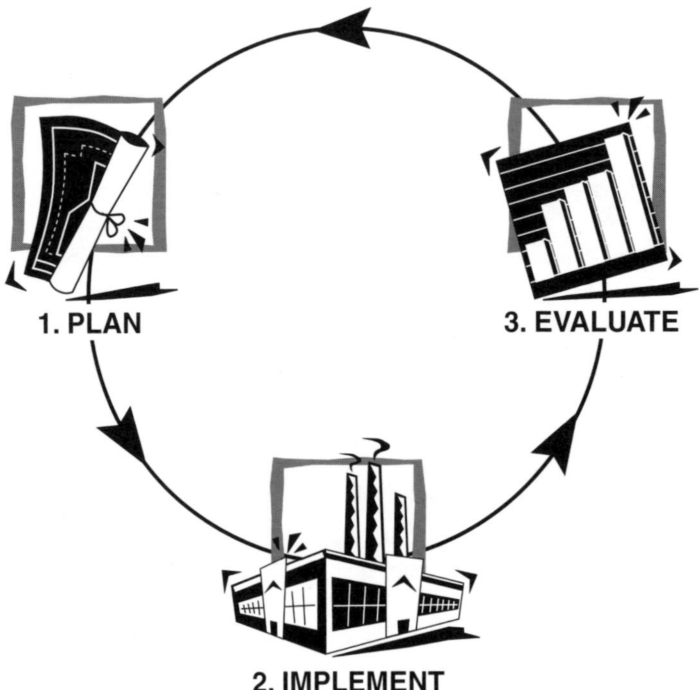

What's so new about the approach? Nothing—until you actually apply it. That's where the series really breaks the mold. Besides telling you how important it is to plan for success in directing your programs, each resource will lead you step-by-step through that planning process. Forms and exercises will help you explore your role and philosophy within the organization, examine your particular needs, and then develop an effective plan of action. In each SportDirector resource these steps are applied specifically to the task at hand. For example, it is essential to assess your needs carefully as you carry out each of your program responsibilities: How you assess promotional needs, however, will differ significantly from how you assess personnel management needs. The series follows the same practical approach to lead you through the implementation and evaluation of your plan.

This approach is possible only because the series authors are experts not only in sport management but also in the specific areas they write about. With the help of the editorial advisory board, these authors translate their knowledge into practical, easy-to-follow recommendations, ready-to-use forms and checklists, and countless practical tips so that you will come away with better ideas for directing your program. The authors also help you take advantage of the latest technology.

New and experienced interscholastic athletic directors alike will find that these resources take into account their widespread responsibilities and limited staff and funding assistance. Directors of Olympic National Governing Body club sport programs and other national and state sport directors will find valuable tools to enhance their efficiency and increase their effectiveness. Students of sport administration will find these resources valuable companions for understanding how to step into the field with confidence to succeed. And all sport directors will find that these tools help them to help the athletes, coaches, parents, and others in their organizational community.

Even more than a leader, you are the architect of your organization's athletic community. As you design and oversee the construction and maintenance of that community, you are in a unique position to ensure that the program achieves a common purpose. The SportDirector Series is conceived not only to help you attend to your everyday duties but also to coalesce your efforts to carry out your program's mission—to make your athletic community the best it can be.

—Jim Kestner

Acknowledgments

During the past four years, this book traveled a variety of paths to become the finished product you now are reading. From the beginning my wife, Suzie, provided encouragement and exercised incredible patience (more than I deserved), helping me keep my head up through all the rewrites and edits. Our children Bradley and Erin knew only that their dad was writing "a book," yet they were as helpful and loving as they could be.

Colleagues at the Michigan High School Athletic Association and at other state associations deserve thanks not only for their support but also for the tidbits of information they provided whenever I asked. Several individuals provided invaluable feedback while this book was in its earliest stages. I especially thank Paul Morgan of the Kalamazoo (Michigan) *Gazette* and Carl Olson of the Battle Creek (Michigan) *Shopper-News*, whose professional counsel and unconditional friendship are truly appreciated.

Other members of the Michigan communications media have helped me, as have colleagues in high schools and college sports information across the Midwest. Although they are too numerous to list individually, they all have earned my special thanks for their contributions of facts and data.

To Chuck Crabb, my friend and former officemate in the athletic department at Indiana University, thanks for a great Foreword. It was an honor to work with you earlier and a pleasure to have you involved now.

Finally, a big *thank you* to various staff members of the Human Kinetics team: Rainer Martens, for his confidence that the ideas expressed in the first draft of this book would be worthwhile to athletic administrators; Jim Kestner, for getting the ball rolling toward the final presentation of these concepts and for assisting again in the final days before the book's publication; Jan Seeley, for being a great editor and inspiring me to fully expand on many ideas to make this text more useful to a wider readership; and Erin Cler, Jan's assistant, for attending to many necessary details.

To all these people and those I may have missed, I thank you for helping me realize a dream with the publication of this book. May God bless you all.

Introduction

Several years ago, while writing a series of short articles about statistics keeping and media relations for a high school coaches' publication, I realized that although many coaches and athletic administrators have been schooled in *Xs* and *Os*, they haven't spent much time learning how to promote their programs properly. Those who take college sport administration courses in promotion and publicity generally specialize in those areas, and no *how to* guides that cater to high school personnel's needs are widely available.

High school promotion, public relations, and sponsorship campaigns are just beginning to grow beyond someone grinding out an occasional press release and the local soft drink distributor underwriting the cost of the football field scoreboard. Many people find high school sponsorships a sell out and feel that prep sports have succumbed to the commercialism that has infiltrated college and professional sport. That is why sizing up your community and school before launching any kind of campaign is critical. The politics of promotion programs differ in every community, but we can still provide you a road map to follow once you have decided to approach promotion as an integral part of your daily operations. You still can maintain the wholesomeness high school sports have enjoyed for years.

We will cover a total promotion program in the chapters ahead. You may not be able to use everything, but by taking bits and pieces, you can fashion something that fits your school's and community's style and needs.

The first part of the book helps you plan for an effective promotion program. This section includes how your organizational and personal promotional philosophies mesh together, how to assess your promotional needs and limitations, and how to develop a comprehensive promotion plan. Chapter 1 deals with the philosophical considerations of promotions such as defining high school sports and their role in the community, and determining how you and your school view promotions.

Chapter 2 is a review of your promotional needs and how to satisfy those needs within your parameters. Simply having the need or desire for a certain type of promotion will not work if you do not have the people or facilities to make it happen.

How to develop your promotion plan is detailed in chapter 3. Promotions are presented here as detailed, year-round considerations, as opposed to the three or four days a year that some organizations devoted to it in the past.

Part II is devoted to building positive public relations, developing print promotions, working with the media, developing special promotions, and selling your program to businesses to underwrite the costs of your promotion program.

Chapter 4 presents public relations as aspects of promoting your program that you control in both your school system and community.

Chapter 5 is devoted to print matter. We look at schedules and game programs to be sold at your events. Your ability to print schedules and programs is based on your available time and resources. Regardless of your situation, this chapter discusses the wide variety of options available and walks you through the production process.

Media is often a four-letter word to athletic administrators and coaches, but because you can't live without them, chapter 6 helps you better understand and live *with* them. We also discuss how to use radio and television to promote your program.

Sometimes, a successful team isn't enough to attract people, especially when students and adults have so many options for filling their leisure time. Chapter 7 discusses several special promotions that you can use for ticketing and entertainment. Learn how to tie activities and target groups into your events to attract spectators once, then keep them coming back.

Finally, a solid promotion program relies on a strong sales effort. Chapter 8 shows you how to develop packages that you can sell in your community to raise additional money with promotional packages.

As a high school sport director, you have responsibility for our most precious commodities—our kids. You are in charge of 14- to 17-year-old men and women at a most impressionable time in their lives. Your sport program provides them with a positive alternative to the negative forces in our society; school sport can unite entire student bodies and communities.

How you promote those youngsters—recognizing them for their achievements—can affect them for a lifetime. This power is in your hands. Use it, and the resources in this book, well.

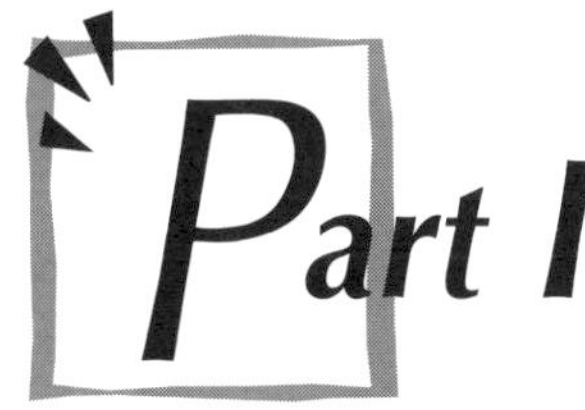

Part I
Planning for Effective Promotion

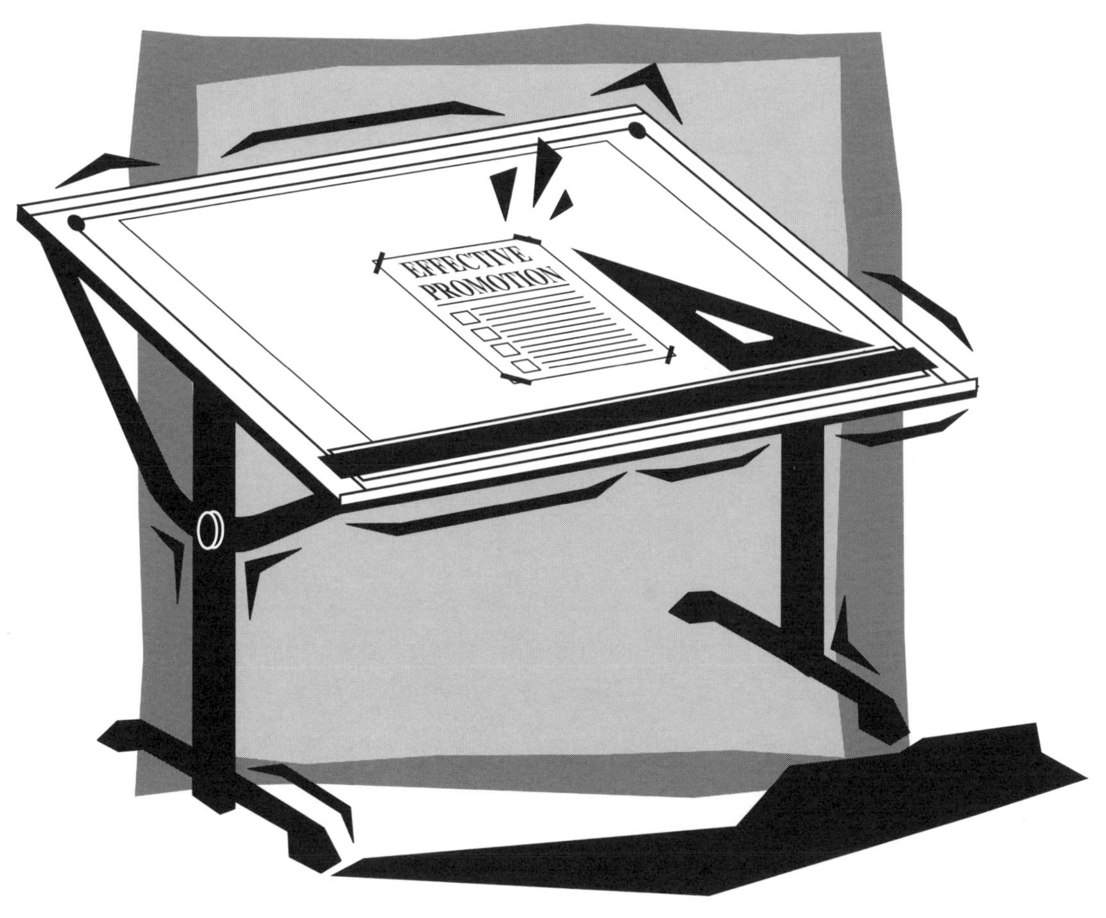

Chapter 1
Understanding Your Role as Sport Director

It is an understatement to say that the tone of a sport program is set at the top. After all, only when a sound philosophy exists at the top does a program achieve success in all areas—including promotion.

A solid organizational philosophy is important so that changes in personnel—which are becoming more frequent in sport—do not adversely affect the organization. Your approach to promotion should build on this philosophy. If no philosophical base for promotion exists, establishing one is an immediate necessity. After you establish that base, you can begin assembling the pieces of an effective promotion program.

This chapter explores your promotional role by helping you to

1. understand personal and organizational philosophies,
2. recognize your role in the organization, and
3. establish promotional goals and objectives.

UNDERSTANDING PERSONAL AND ORGANIZATIONAL PHILOSOPHIES

The philosophy behind educational athletics begins with the notion that school sport exists for different reasons than other sport activities. Purposes of athletics range from providing entertainment to training participants for elite competition, but high school sport is the only level of athletics that exists primarily to educate students. Strive never to lose this ideal; keep it as a guiding light for your work to promote your program.

Understanding that high school sport is part of a youngster's learning process will help you develop a promotional philosophy that is compatible with that educational focus.

Benefits of Educational Athletics

For more than 5.5 million young men and women, educational athletics complement the classroom learning experience. Kids voluntarily work hour after hour to better themselves in these co-curricular programs. Well-run programs teach young people that life is more than wins and losses, develop character, and stress lifelong values, such as ethics, integrity, and respect. You can use these and the following traits to help sell your program in the community.

Student Benefits

Many things in education are "outcome oriented." That is, test scores and other measuring sticks are used to determine how effective our classroom programs are. School sport has its own set of gauges to show its value in the community.

Student sport participation varies by school size and location. However, school athletic programs frequently involve 75 percent of the student body; no other activity involves as many students.

Several national studies show that athletic program participants have better grade point averages than general student populations. These studies show that athletes post better grades during the sport season, that multi-sport athletes do better in the classroom than single-sport athletes, and that athletic participation may be a strong indicator of one's success in adult life. Discipline and attendance problems are fewer among athletes, and they also tend to be less involved with controlled substances like alcohol and drugs.

In addition to these figures, many students say that sport participation helps them better organize their time among school activities, classroom responsibilities, and other interests. These programs also give students a reason to go to school. Youngsters feel a need to belong, leading some to turn to gangs. Athletic programs can help fulfill this need by encouraging involvement of as many kids as possible.

School Activities—Promoting Achievement

- Student athletes maintain higher grade point averages (2.84 GPA) than other students (2.68 GPA) and are absent from school fewer days (7.44 compared with 8.76).

  —Minnesota State High School League Study (1983)

- As a group, students who do not participate in sports have a 2.39 grade point average, whereas those who participate in one sport score a 2.61 GPA and those who are active in two sports achieve a 2.82 GPA.

  —Iowa High School Athletic Association Study (1981)

- Students who participate in activities average 3.32 GPA, while nonparticipants average 2.48 GPA. Furthermore, participants miss an average of 4.9 days per year of school (including .7 for activities), while nonparticipants miss 10.8 days per year.

  —North Dakota High School Activities Association Study (1986)

- Grade point averages of athletes improve the grade point average of the general student population in every school and in every category (in-season, off-season, minority).

  —South Bend, IN, Community Schools Study (1991)

- "High activity" students (those involved in four or more activities) averaged a 3.05 GPA, whereas "low activity" students averaged a 2.54 GPA.

  —Indiana University Study (1983)

- Based on 4.0 GPA as 100%, athletes averaged 86%, compared with 79% for the general population. Athletes averaged four absences, compared with seven for the general population. Eleven percent of athletes had discipline referrals, compared with twenty-five percent of the general population. No athletes dropped out of school, whereas 3.7% of the general population were dropouts.

—Randolph, NC, County Schools Study of 5 high schools (1990–91)

- University of Chicago research suggests:

—By a two-to-one margin for males and a three-to-one margin for females, student athletes do better in school, do not drop out, and have a better chance to get through college.

—Student athletes take average and above-average courses.

—Student athletes' parents are more involved with the educational process.

—Student athletes tend to focus more on long-term life accomplishments than on short-term goals.

—Student athletes are more self-assured.

—92% of sport participants do not use drugs.

—School Sports & Education

- Ninety-five percent of school principals believe activities programs contribute to the development of "school spirit" among the student body.

—Indiana University Study (1985)

- The GPA for Manistee High School students on the whole is 2.399, compared with 3.128 for athletes (49% of the student body).

—Manistee, MI, Area Schools Study (1993)

- In their youth, 95% of Fortune 500 executives had participated in school athletics (only 47% of them were in the National Honor Society).

—Fortune Magazine (1987)

- Extracurricular participation is a school's best predictor of an adult's success.

—*Fulfilling Lives: Paths to Maturity and Success* (Douglas H. Heath, based on 40-year survey, 1991)

School Benefits

Athletic programs also bring many positive effects to schools. Rallying around the athletic program provides a positive outlet for students and improves morale for students and staff. In 1981–82, the public high schools in Pontiac, Michigan, endured a year without athletics. Said one coach, "It was depressing. The atmosphere was different. There was silence in the halls, and school spirit was dead."

Athletic programs interact with many school groups, including cheerleaders, pom pom squads, trainers, managers, statisticians, yearbook and newspaper staffs, radio and television crews, bands, pep clubs, and others. Well-run athletic programs strive to integrate all these groups. Expanding other students' educational experiences through their work with athletics puts a positive spin on the community's perception of the school program.

Community Benefits

When your athletic program runs on all cylinders, benefits to the community abound. A priceless benefit is enhanced community spirit: The town uses the athletic program as a rallying point, a selling point, and an intense source of community pride. Regardless of whether your teams have winning seasons, athletic events provide wholesome, controlled activities for youngsters. During contests and post-contest functions, parents and civic leaders know that youth are in safe hands.

In a 1993 teleconference sponsored by the Michigan High School Athletic Association, a member of the Lansing Waverly Public School Board emphasized this point: "I would much rather see our kids in our football stadiums on a Friday night or the basketball arenas on Friday nights actively participating in well-organized activities than hanging or chilling at the mall, and I'm afraid that if we don't give them supervised activities, they will find something else to do that may not always be in the best interests of the community."

Additionally, this controlled activity provides low-cost entertainment for families in your area. A family of four attending a high school football game pays approximately $15 to $20 to get in—even less in some communities. One ticket to a major college football game can cost over $20, and will never provide the same family atmosphere. People like enjoyable and modestly-priced entertainment, and high

A Cost Comparison

The following is a comparison of what it costs for a family of four to attend a typical high school athletic event, a movie, and a college football game.

	High school event	Movie	College football game
Tickets	$16.00	$20.00	$100.00
Parking	-0-	-0-	$5.00
Program (1)	$1.00	-0-	$3.00
Popcorn (4)	$3.00	$8.00	$6.00
Hot dogs (4)	$4.00	$7.00	$7.00
Soft drinks (4)	$3.00	$5.00	$6.00
Totals	$27.00	$40.00	$127.00*

*Excluding souvenirs

schools offer that product at a time when movies, concerts, and other activities are becoming cost prohibitive to attend regularly.

Your athletic program also helps sell the community to potential newcomers and retain existing homeowners. If all else between neighboring communities is equal, a solid school system with a well-run athletics and activities program will sway a person making a decision about where to buy a home.

WHY HIGH SCHOOL ATHLETICS ARE UNIQUE

High school athletics are the last bastion of educational sports, and encouraging learning in a variety of situations should take precedence over promoting elitism and specialization. Your athletic programs should be open to all students. Many school districts are now running no-cut programs from the junior high to the varsity level, and some field several teams in each grade at the junior high/middle school level. Although no-cut programs are not always practical at the varsity level, some schools have expanded rosters, allowing, for example, more than the traditional 15 players in basketball.

When more students are involved in the program, playing becomes *fun*. A recent study by the Youth Sports Institute of Michigan State University found that having fun was the number one reason boys and girls played sports at the high school level and that winning ranked well down the list. Having more kids involved also means more opportunities for teaching values through school sports.

A well-run school athletic program places education first: Studies are for everybody, including the team's stars; excessive travel and participation in lengthy tournaments are avoided; and fund-raisers involving athletes are minimized. It also promotes broad-based support with a blanket booster club operation rather than independent booster clubs, which generally compete with each other.

DEFINING PHILOSOPHIES

Even educational sport philosophies vary by community and individual, and some sport directors, communities, and organizations favor a particular sport or gender. An organization's sport philosophy also impacts its approach to promotion, and sport directors, regardless of their own perspectives, must work within that framework. Sport directors can influence an organizational philosophy, but these changes can only occur over time. Figure 1.1 depicts the philosophical hierarchy of an organization and its sport director.

I. Organizational philosophy
   A. Purpose of sport programs in educational process
   B. Value of promotion as part of the process

II. Sport director's philosophy
   A. Uses most positive values of program's purpose to identify selling points
   B. Determines needs within programs
   C. Determines what is and is not acceptable to school and community for specific promotions
   D. Uses personal preferences to determine specific promotions

Figure 1.1 Promotional philosophical hierarchy.

Organizational Philosophies

Your organizational philosophy should be established by the principal or superintendent and approved by the local school board. It should emphasize the positive aspects of sport as an integral part of the educational process.

The organizational philosophy provides you with general guidelines for promotion, setting the tone, not necessarily specific parts of the program. Specifics are likely left for you to develop. Organizational philosophy as a whole will encompass issues like

- making the program available to the few or to the masses,
- the role of fund-raising in the community, and
- the level of commercialization that will be tolerated via business and corporate support.

Personal Philosophies

Your personal promotional philosophies, even if you have not given them much thought before, have already evolved, in part because of the marketing blitz we experience daily. You already know what you find appealing and appalling in advertising pitches and promotion programs. Watching television and attending organized events from music concerts to festivals, expose you to marketing efforts and promotional programs.

Take a few minutes to fill out Form 1.1, listing the range of promotions you have been exposed to in the past 90 days. You may be surprised by what you compile.

Next, break that list down into three categories, the first being promotions you really liked, the second being those you disliked because of substance or style, and the third noting those promotions for which you had neither strong positive nor negative feelings. Once you complete your list, you have gone far toward discovering your personal promotional philosophy.

For example, if the idea of a sponsor's name preceding the name of an event (e.g., The Sports Shoe Junior Widgetball Nationals) sits well with you, you might explore such an option for one of your events. If you find the revolving signs that have become courtside fixtures in many major league basketball arenas repulsive, then you might resist offering signage opportunities at your venues.

You are now ready to refine your personal philosophy, breaking it into the components of promotion we discuss in the coming chapters: public relations, print items, media opportunities, pregame

Form 1.1 Rating Promotions You've Been Exposed To

To assist you in developing your personal promotional philosophy, list in the left-hand column of this form some of the different promotions you have been exposed to. Indicate your preference for each method by placing the appropriate letter after each one.

Promotions	Preference L=Liked method; N=Neutral; D=Disliked method
____________________	__________
____________________	__________
____________________	__________
____________________	__________
____________________	__________

and in-game promotions, fund-raising drives, advertising, and sponsorships. You also need to integrate those thoughts with the values you regard as essential in educational sport.

Combining Organization/Personal Philosophies

Now that you have examined a potential promotional hierarchy for your organization, as well as considered your personal views on promotion, you need to put that information to use. Form 1.2 asks you a series of questions to help you focus on the sport philosophy of your organization, the role of promotion, and the responsibilities of your position. Form 1.3 asks key questions about your personal promotional philosophy, helping you write your philosophy, then tie it to the elements of Form 1.2 .

Putting It in Writing

Completing these forms is a critical step toward developing your personal and organizational philosophies. After you write your philosophy, you will be ready to create goals, programs, and proposals to sell your ideas. How well you communicate on paper is as important as any verbal communication.

RECOGNIZING THE SPORT DIRECTOR'S ROLE IN PROMOTION

The promotion ball is literally in your hands in many school districts. Once you understand your personal and organizational philosophies, you need to develop a general diagram to determine your role in athletic promotion. This diagram should be reviewed by other administrators in your organization, and possibly by its board.

The form of that general diagram will depend on how much support you have. In some schools, the sport director has the luxury of an assistant who could take on any portion of the promotion responsibilities, or a consistent, competent umbrella booster club that reports on its activities regularly. But in most cases, it is the director who is the liaison to the athletes, their parents, and the community.

Figure 1.2 presents a general organizational ladder. When we discuss the actual delegation of responsibilities in chapter 3, you will see how this structure works.

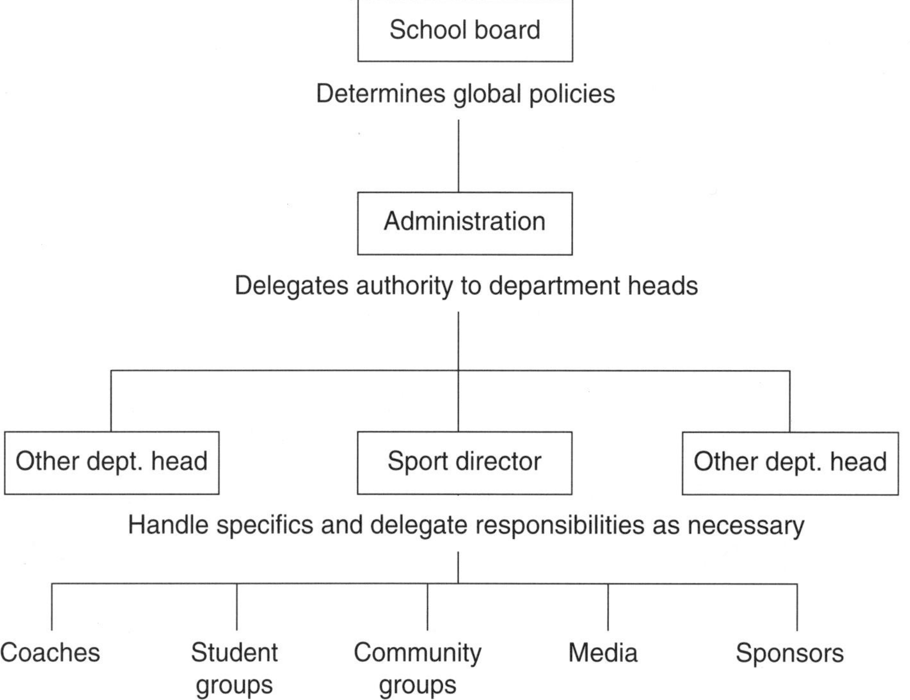

Figure 1.2 Identifying your promotional role/position.

Form 1.2 Your Organization's Promotional Philosophy

To help you understand your organization's approach to promotions, answer the following questions.

1. What is the organization's philosophy regarding sports?

2. How do promotions interface with that philosophy?

3. What kind of promotions does the organization desire?

4. What kind of promotions are not desired by the organization?

5. What does the organization perceive the role of the sport director to be in the promotion process?

6. Based on your previous answers, what potential for conflict exists in the following areas:

a. within the organization

b. in the community

7. How can those conflicts be resolved?

Form 1.3 Your Personal Promotional Philosophy

To help you understand your personal approach to promotions and how it relates to your organization's promotional philosophy, answer the following questions.

1. What is my personal philosophy regarding sports?

2. What is my personal philosophy regarding promotions?

3. How does my philosophy impact the promotions process?

4. Given the above, what potential for conflict exists in the following areas:

a. within the organization

b. in the community

5. How can those conflicts be resolved?

ESTABLISHING PROMOTIONAL GOALS AND OBJECTIVES

Based on your organizational and personal philosophies, you will need to assess the following before setting your promotional goals and objectives:

- The general direction and resources you receive from your administration and board
- The composition of your community (urban, suburban, small town, rural) and its resources
- Your own schedule (full-time versus part-time director responsibilities)

The next chapter helps you to evaluate your situation. Once you complete these assessments, you use them as follows to develop your goals and objectives:

1. To determine and communicate the primary purposes of the athletic program
2. To seek student body involvement in the program
3. To seek community involvement as program sponsors and spectators

Summary

To better understand your promotional role as a sport director,

1. consider how philosophies for promoting high school sport in general begin with an understanding that these activities are educational in nature, with far-reaching benefits to schools, athletes, the general student body, and the community;
2. recognize that educational athletics differ from sports at the college and professional levels;
3. use the organization's philosophy toward athletics and promotion to provide the base for you to develop your philosophy;
4. realize that personal philosophy is more easily developed than you might think, depending on your tastes in marketing and advertising;
5. put your philosophy in writing to provide a base you can depend on as you *sell* your program to the school, community, potential sponsors, and advertisers;
6. understand that the organization and top-level administration set a general tone for promotion, and you work from a much longer, more specific list; and
7. analyze several factors to determine your promotional goals and objectives.

Chapter 2
Assessing Your Needs

Numerous elements influence your program. This chapter identifies those elements by

1. sizing up your organization by identifying your programs,
2. determining the promotional needs of those different programs, and
3. balancing those needs with your available resources.

Just as a marketing plan for a department store is often built around a regularly scheduled inventory, assessing the direction your promotion program should take is based on compiling a list of your program components and the factors that influence it.

The plan a store develops is influenced by the community type and the store's needs. Build your promotion program the same way. Without knowing specifically what type of marketplace you are working in, you can compile all the best promotional ideas you have seen work in other communities—and fall flat on your face. The key word here is *other*. Because it worked in that *other* community is no guarantee it will work in yours.

SIZING UP YOUR PROGRAM

This is not as easy as saying you have 10 boys' sports and 11 girls' sports involving 467 kids. Head counting is a fair place to start, but some people miss the big picture because they don't get below the surface of those initial numbers. Breaking down those numbers into categories will give you the best view of the big picture for sizing up your program.

- Identify by season the number of sports you have and the different levels of teams fielded in each (i.e., varsity, junior varsity, freshman, middle school or junior high, and elementary). If your duties extend into the intramural or club area, you will also need to list the number of programs, teams, and individuals involved.
- Identify the number of individuals involved, including administrators, coaches, athletes, and support personnel.
- Identify the various clubs and organizations that affiliate with your sport program. These can be student and nonstudent groups.

Identifying the Size and Scope of Your Program

You could use an organizational tree to construct a view of your big picture, putting the overall program at the top of the structure, then branching out and down to each sport, its different levels, and affiliated organizations. The lower reaches of the chart are spectators and other outside groups you are trying to reach through your promotion program.

Form 2.1 is a sample fill-in-the-blank concept from which you could build an organizational tree. By identifying the various levels of your program, you will get an accurate picture of what you're working with.

Identifying the Number of Individuals Involved

Breaking down the overall number of teams also requires that you figure in everyone who is involved. Administrators, coaches, athletes, and members of the support staff, be they managers, trainers, statisticians, or others, are just as critical.

Form 2.1 Sizing Up the Organization

To help you assess the makeup of your community, complete this form. This will give you the background information necessary to assist you in developing your promotion plan.

Community population: ______________________________

Type of community: ______________________________
(rural, urban, suburban, industrial, bedroom, etc.)

Student population

High school

male/female: ______________________________

Junior high/middle school

male/female: ______________________________

Elementary

male/female: ______________________________

Student-athletes

9th grade - male/female: ______________________________

10th grade - male/female: ______________________________

11th grade - male/female: ______________________________

12th grade - male/female: ______________________________

Number of interscholastic sports (male/female): ______________________________

The following is a breakdown to be used and modified for each sport and level.

Sport: ______________________________

Varsity participants

Coaches: ______________________________

Support personnel: ______________________________

Home games per game attendance: ______________________________

Away games per game attendance: ______________________________

Sub-varsity participants

Coaches: ______________________________

Support personnel: ______________________________

Home games per game attendance: ______________________________

Away games per game attendance: ______________________________

Freshman participants

Coaches: ______________________________

Support personnel: ______________________________

Home games per game attendance: ______________________________

Away games per game attendance: ______________________________

Junior high/middle school participants

Coaches: ______________________________

Support personnel: ______________________________

Home games per game attendance: ______________________________

Away games per game attendance: ______________________________

The following is a breakdown to be used and modified for each club and organization.

Name of group: ______________________________

School or community group: ______________________________

Number of members: ______________________________

Purpose of group: ______________________________

President, director, or faculty advisor: ______________________________

Many believe, for example, that a varsity basketball team runs on 15 players. In reality, that number can grow well into the 20s when you count everyone involved. Those hidden people are vital to your program. Statistics from the National Federation of State High School Associations show that school athletic programs involve up to 75 percent of the student body in some manner. Those nonathletic positions are just as much a part of the team as uniformed players.

Identifying Clubs and Organizations

Providing a positive educational sport experience is not limited just to players. Individuals who affiliate with athletic teams are also responsible for the success of the promotion program. Cheerleaders, honor students, and a variety of other groups can become part of the program. Outside the student body, support groups take their forms as booster clubs and community service organizations, such as the Lions and Kiwanis. In many school districts, adult groups work behind the scenes, involving even more people.

You might think that by the time you finish figuring out how many people are affiliated with the program, few spectators will remain. But turning to your financial reports, you can determine the average attendance for a sport, a season, or even a rivalry. All these factors tell you whom to get involved and how many people to expect. This is also the data from which you will draw the information that helps sell your program to the community.

After examining your organization, look at your community. The type of school you are working for, be it urban, suburban, small town, or rural, will affect the tree, as well as your promotional needs and available resources.

DETERMINING YOUR PROMOTIONAL NEEDS

In chapter 1, you determined your promotion program philosophy. Your next step is to determine your needs for

- your interscholastic sport program at its different levels,
- your intramural sport program,
- your club sport or activities program, and
- the special events you conduct for any or all of these program offerings.

This section takes the approach that you may not only be responsible for your interscholastic athletic program, but for other participation programs as well. In some schools, for example, the athletic director also is an activities director.

Form 2.2 helps you to analyze your organization and community to determine your promotional needs and to balance those needs with your available resources. Interscholastic programs probably deserve your primary attention, appearing more tangible to the community. But promotion can also involve intramural and club sport. A sponsor may provide trophies for an intramural basketball or flag football tournament or help underwrite some of the costs for a club sport that is not sponsored as an interscholastic activity. Recognizing the achievements of students involved in these programs is also important. Special events, ranging from an annual wrestling, track, or volleyball invitational to major fund-raisers like pancake dinners, offer far-reaching benefits for the various programs your school sponsors.

BALANCING YOUR NEEDS AND RESOURCES

Items 5 through 10 on Form 2.2 can be likened to reconciling your checkbook every month. You balance needs and limitations in a plan that prioritizes the promotion projects you will undertake. Consider developing a short- and long-term program, in which, as you become comfortable with your schedule and limitations, new elements are added each year.

Determining Your Limitations

We've discussed collecting a lot of data to help you determine your promotional priorities. Use this data to identify program strengths and challenges and to establish a plan for facing those challenges.

The first factor determining your limitations is your philosophy. As we discussed in chapter 1, your philosophy synthesizes organization and community ideas with your own. You need to establish a financial plan that reflects your philosophy: Determine whether your facilities and equipment will accommodate your ideas, and whether you have adequate personnel and time.

Philosophical Limitations

Your organizational and personal philosophies represent your first set of promotional boundaries, and limitations may range from very free to very restrictive. Taking your philosophy to one extreme, imagine that your organization wants to make every home event a happening. Your orders are to attract sponsors for halftime shootouts, giveaways, and an annual appearance by a professional sport mascot, as

Form 2.2 Determining Promotional Needs and Limitations

This form will help you determine the potential for promoting a sport, and some of the limitations you may face. Fill in the blanks that follow:

1. Sport or event: ______________________________
2. Schedule or event date: ______________________________
3. Location: ______________________________
4. Previous year's attendance: ______________________________
   (break down by game if a season)
5. Maximum seating capacity: ______________________________
6. Promotion possibilities: ______________________________
   ____
   ____

   Public relations: ______________________________
   ____

   Print promotions: ______________________________
   ____

   Mass media: ______________________________
   ____

   Special promotions: ______________________________
   ____

   Corporate sponsorship: ______________________________
   ____
7. Specific needs for this sport or event: ______________________________
   ____
   ____
   ____
8. Available general funding (internal sources): ______________________________
   ____
   ____
9. Potential outside funding (tickets, concessions, sponsors, advertising):
   ____
   ____
   ____

10. Facility and equipment considerations: ______________________________
____
____

11. Facility and equipment limitations: ______________________________
____
____

12. Personnel and time considerations: ______________________________
____
____

13. Personnel and time limitations: ______________________________
____
____

14. Conclusions: ______________________________
____
____

well as to recognize sponsors every way possible. Signage is not a problem; nor is renaming the annual baseball tournament, originally named for a former long-time coach, after the sponsor.

In this instance, your philosophy meshes well with what the administration wants. Before you became an athletic director, you played professional sports, and signs, gimmicks, endorsements, and promotions were part of your daily life.

Your philosophy is one where anything goes, and your plan is laced with multiple sponsors and massive cross promotion among events. It resembles what you see in a major sports arena on any given day.

Now consider a second example. Your administration believes that school sports should not depend on the type of corporate involvement a local college exhibits (illustrated in the first example). The organization follows a very traditional approach—a little advertising to help pay for programs and schedule cards, nothing too modern.

Now imagine that your personal philosophy does not differ from the first example. As you attempt to assemble your promotional package, you will find yourself at odds with the organization. You may try to find every crack in the organization's armor and exploit those few promotion opportunities to their fullest. Your philosophical limitations will be affected by their alignment with your organization. Fewer areas of conflict will facilitate your ability to establish your philosophical boundaries.

Refer back to Forms 1.1 and 1.3 (pages 7 and 11 respectively) as you analyze your philosophical limitations.

Attitude Example

It is not uncommon to encounter others who disagree with you about the benefits of sponsored programs. One school administrator who was asked to judge applications in a sponsor-funded scholarship contest rejected the invitation stating that the only party benefitting from the program was the sponsor.

As you determine your philosophical limitations, differing opinions will dictate the need for you to publicly defend your philosophy. Be prepared to do this in a polite manner within your community.

Financial Limitations

Your next task is arranging the finances to make your program fly. Your organization has probably given you some seed money to print the various materials you will need to sell your ideas. Once the seed money is gone, you need to raise additional funds. Promotions must fund themselves and make a profit to help defray the costs of putting a game on the playing surface. Successful fund-raising is a key component of your promotional scheme. Getting community monies to help underwrite promotions is essential.

Facility and Equipment Limitations

From the entrance of your football stadium to the look of your scoreboard and sound of your public address system, your facilities and equipment are key ingredients of your promotional program. The greatest facilities challenges appear on older campuses, where some updating of the physical plant may be necessary to assist you in executing your promotions. New venues, from major sports arenas to the local gymnasium or football field, are being designed more for spectators, who should be attracted to everything, not forced into the ritual of fighting to reach the concession stand or some other amenity. If faced with physical challenges, or real life lemons, the adage says "Make lemonade." Take your physical plant to its limits to help you promote your program.

For example, if your program sales or concessions are in an out-of-the-way location, you may have trouble selling enough programs at an event for a giveaway in the third quarter for which the public address announcer reads the number imprinted on a sponsor's ad. That public address system had better sound clean as those numbers are read.

But you know that the system is old and the sound is not clear. What can you do in lieu of upgrading the system? You can time your promotion so that cheerleaders, band members, and other key administrators know to be quiet at the time the promotional announcement is read. Or place posters at the concession stand with the winning number.

Possible solutions for selling programs might include the use of program sellers who move through the stands during the pregame to sell programs. Placing a portable concessions trailer in a more accessible and visible area could be a solution to the inaccessibility of the permanent booth.

Likewise, if your football field does not have a fence around it, you cannot hang promotional banners for a game's sponsor in a highly-visible location. You may also need a scoreboard that permits you to attach signage.

Be creative in finding solutions to such dilemmas. Use props to support signage near the sidelines and end zones (a tactic effectively used in the World Cup). The press box or the top of the bleacher railings can also be used to hang signage.

Personnel and Time Limitations

Like a play diagrammed on a chalkboard, no promotional plan will work if you lack the personnel and time to execute it. Try to find that one administrator in your building who wants to volunteer time to assist you with promotion. If your promotion program is successful, you might provide the incentive of remuneration. Your booster club leaders are other potential operatives.

Your board or administration should give you a short, general list of how the promotion program should run. If not, ask! Your list becomes more detailed as you plot things out, and those assigned to execute the plans for individual sports or special events have the most detailed (and possibly longest) lists to work from.

Should Have Said No!

Cathy's organization was hosting a tournament that planned to expand to a two-day event. The publicity director of an athletic department, Cathy volunteered to assist with typing the tournament results. Knowing the event's history of not distributing results to the media in a timely manner, she thought her assisting was the right thing to do.

Shortly after she took on the responsibility of typing results, Cathy was asked to type a variety of other tasks that ranged from names on scorecards to pairings and a program for the second day of the tournament. This all took priority over her publicity responsibilites of getting the results out to the media.

After one year of being thus used and abused, Cathy made sure to include other people for the functions she no longer volunteered to do.

Sport directors generally hope to avoid offending internal or external groups, and occasionally say yes to a request or promotional idea, knowing full well they lack the time, personnel, or facilities to execute the project. Knowing when to say no is important to avoid bogging yourself down. Remember that you can often change no to yes without adverse effects on your efforts. The opposite is not true.

Building a Plan To Fund Promotional Efforts

Sponsorships are specifically covered in chapter 8. However, a plan to raise money to cover the costs of your promotional efforts may be more critical in your initial year than the promotions themselves. You may also find that only a portion of your efforts may come to fruition in that first year. However, instead of feeling discouraged, use it as the base by which you can show your school and community where you've been and where you want to go with your promotion program.

Summary

To help you analyze your promotional needs and limitations, you should

1. determine the exact size of your program and its promotional potential;
2. identify the individuals, clubs, and organizations that affiliate with various programs;
3. determine promotional needs; and
4. find the critical balance between those needs and available resources, determining limitations according to philosophy, finances, facilities, equipment, personnel, and time.

Chapter 3
Developing a Promotion Plan

To twist a Vince Lombardi quote, promotion is not a sometimes thing; it's an all-the-time thing. Promotions during the Lombardi era were generally limited to professional sports. Many of us may remember trekking to a professional baseball game as youngsters on one of the promotion days of the season. It was usually a big giveaway day, and we would take home a bat, a hat, or perhaps a plastic batting helmet. Our new treasure displayed the team's genuine logo and the manufacturer's logo in an appropriate size and location.

On her first trip to a major league baseball game one recent summer, a youngster had a plastic encased baseball thrust into her hands as she walked through the gate. The ball was imprinted with player autographs, but the signatures were dwarfed—not by the manufacturer's logo but by a logo of the promotion sponsor. This youngster still treasures her baseball, proudly displaying it on her bedroom dresser.

Thirty years ago, a team picked three or four promotion days and anticipated that with enough mention of those promotions on radio broadcasts, occasional televised contests, pocket and poster schedules, and in newspapers, the cost of the item given away would be easily recouped in ticket sales.

Today, there is a promotion for nearly every home contest, with multiple mention on daily radio and television broadcasts, always accompanied by a sponsor. Any newspaper mention of the promotion comes from the sponsor's purchase of advertising space as part of the package, and the sponsor receives more attention than the giveaway item.

The primary difference between these promotions is the intricate planning that goes into making modern promotions successful. Another major difference is that promotional efforts used to be handled by a business or public relations director. Today, professional teams employ entire marketing staffs, and major colleges have at least one full-time person assigned to such tasks.

You probably do not have the luxury of a trained body to handle your promotions, but planning is still essential for putting your promotional program into place. You want to avoid falling into the common hit-and-miss promotions trap, only doing something for the occasional *big* game, usually in a more spontaneous rather than planned manner.

In this chapter, you will learn

1. how to keep and use records in your promotion program,
2. how to involve key members of your organization, and
3. how to plan to evaluate your promotion program.

KEEPING AND USING RECORDS

Unlike statistical forms for sports, there is no uniform record-keeping book to help you plan and track promotions. Forms 2.1 and 2.2 (see pp. 14 and 17 respectively) take a global view of each sport and its specific features. Some of the forms described in this chapter resemble 15-month calendars, similar to popular day planner/organizers. Depending on your needs, you might use some commercially available forms with no modifications.

These forms can be used to centralize data for your general athletic and promotion-specific functions. Most of this data is generally available in your files. For example, you can use rosters from your different sports to determine the number of participants, coaches, and other support staff; and your business records should include attendance figures.

Developing Policy Manuals, Time Lines, Checklists, and Forms

Your policy manual—your road map to how your promotion program should operate—has been developed to reflect your personal and organizational philosophies.

It should state your organization's approach to promotion and describe how promotion plans will be fulfilled (see outline in Figure 3.1).

I. Organization mission statement—sport programs

II. The role of promotion in the sport program

III. Global promotion efforts
   - A. Public relations
   - B. Print promotions
   - C. Media relations
   - D. Special event promotions
   - E. Advertising/marketing/sponsorship

IV. Types of promotion programs—by sport
   - A. Varsity
     1. Public relations
     2. Print promotions
     3. Media relations
     4. Special event promotions
     5. Advertising/marketing/sponsorship
   - B. Sub-Varsity

V. Personnel considerations

VI. Facility considerations

Figure 3.1 Policy manual.

Time lines are critical. Just as you must develop timetables for practices and games, your schedule for promotion requires its own yearlong calendar and should probably differ from the typical school calendar by about three months. To plan and execute promotions properly you need to make decisions at about the same time you establish the budget for the coming year. Here's a simplified sample:

- **April**—develop master calendar and budget for coming school-year promotions.
- **May**—begin making sponsorship contacts; solicit printing and other bids.
- **June/July**—execute summer fund-raising events; finish sponsorship contacts; award bids; submit copy for initial fall print promotions.
- **August**—execute additional fund-raisers; initiate public relations plans; accept delivery of fall printed promotional items; begin submitting copy for fall souvenir programs.
- **September**—execute event promotions as scheduled; accept delivery of fall souvenir programs.

- **October**—execute event promotions as scheduled; submit copy for initial winter print promotions.
- **November**—execute contingency promotions for fall statewide tournaments as teams advance; accept delivery of initial winter print promotions; submit copy for winter souvenir programs.
- **December**—accept delivery of winter souvenir programs.
- **January**—execute event promotions as scheduled; execute midyear fund-raiser; execute winter public relations efforts.
- **February**—execute event promotions as scheduled; begin submitting copy for initial spring print promotions.
- **March**—execute contingency promotions for winter statewide tournaments as teams advance; accept delivery of initial spring print promotions; submit copy for spring souvenir programs.
- **April**—initiate spring public relations plans; accept delivery of spring printed promotional items; accept delivery of spring souvenir programs. Begin overlap with planning calendar for upcoming school year.
- **May**—execute event promotions as scheduled; year-end fund-raiser.
- **June**—execute contingency promotions for spring statewide tournaments as teams advance.

A 15-month plan probably best describes what happens when you assemble your promotion calendar. Your final calendar will become more detailed as you add checklists and other forms to assist you in developing and executing these projects.

Your checklists detail each project with step-by-step directions. These checklists will likely cover the promotion categories explored in the remaining chapters—public relations, print promotions, mass media promotions, special promotions, and obtaining sponsorships. Other forms will accompany your checklist. Each form will break down the categories on the checklist. For example, if planning a giveaway night, you can develop forms to list potential sponsors, as well as vendors who could provide the giveaway item. Both would include a contact history, similar to what good salespeople maintain about their clients.

A Sample Promotion Plan Form

This form can be modified for any type of promotion. In this case, the form is being used to obtain "terrible towels" to be given away at an upcoming contest.

Promotion Plan Outline

Project: terrible towels

Reference category: giveaways

Date: March 1

Sport/event: boys/girls basketball games with Elwood

Location: Alumni Gymnasium

Completion date: Feb. 25

Project description: Print athletic logo on 1,000 towels to be passed out to student body for potential league championship games.

Idea (development, drawings): Blue ink on a yellow towel. Mrs. Simons' art class will come up with the design.

Contacts: Bob Watkins at Watkins and Son Advertising Specialities (555-5555) for towels. Must receive artwork by Feb. 1 to complete in time. Harry Richards at Burger World (555-2222) will underwrite cost for a logo on the towels. Burger World will also offer Big Burger discount if party brings in towel after game.

Costs: Towels are $.25 per unit for 1,000. Total cost is $400 plus set-up fees of approximately $50.

With these forms you would also include a description or actual sample of the giveaway item, a breakdown of costs, samples of the artwork to appear on the giveaway item, names of sponsors to help underwrite the giveaway, how those sponsors would be recognized for their contribution, and notes about the actual execution of the promotion (e.g., giveaways at the gate, items placed on seats, and items thrown into the crowd by cheerleaders).

Form 3.1 is a generic checklist for a promotion project. This form may be modified depending on the type of promotion you are running.

Form 3.1 Promotion Checklist (Generic)

Use this form to guide you in the promotions you may wish to engage in for a specific sport or event.

Sport: ____________________

Level: ____________________

Date: ____________________

Opponent/type of meet: ____________________

____

Number of teams: ____________________

Venue and capacity: ____________________

Objective of promotion: ____________________

____

____

____

Promotion avenues (check off and attach forms for all that apply):

- ❑ Public relations
- ❑ Print
- ❑ Media relations
- ❑ Special promotions
- ❑ Advertising/marketing/sponsorship

Individual or group involvement (list here and attach responsibility forms):

____

____

____

____

Key contacts: ____________________

____

____

____

____

A 1-Month Focus

The 15-month calendar gives us a general overview of a promotion program. Here we take 1 month and break it down by weeks:

- November—month overview:

  Execute contingency promotions for fall statewide tournaments as teams advance; accept delivery of initial winter print promotions; submit copy for winter souvenir programs.

- Weekly overview:

  November 1–7—prepare and print good luck posters for first-round football and volleyball tournament dates; plan Friday pep assembly for football and volleyball teams; begin contingency plan for trip to state football and volleyball finals with booster clubs.

  November 8–14—prepare for second week of state tournaments; submit hard copy for winter sports souvenir programs; take pictures of winter teams for souvenir programs; continue contingency plans to state finals with booster clubs.

  November 15–21—prepare for third week of state tournaments; proof typeset copy for winter sports souvenir programs; submit photos for souvenir programs; finalize contingency plans to state finals with booster clubs.

  November 22–28—prepare for state finals if teams are still in tournaments; look at final proofs of winter programs and approve for printing; prepare for post-state tournament celebrations and promotional items.

Gathering Information on Past Promotions

If you can gather records about attendance at past events and promotions associated with them, do it. Any paperwork you can refer to, as opposed to relying on memories, will get you off to a better start.

Some sources may include athletic department and booster club financial reports from previous years. Those records may help you track attendance, promotions executed, costs, and possibly the organization behind those promotions. You may only find year-end statements, or you may find event-by-event or sport-by-sport breakdowns. With the rapid turnover in the sport director position at some schools, you may be lucky to find anything.

"We Could've Sold 500 More"

When preparing to order souvenir t-shirts and sweatshirts for upcoming state tournaments, the staff member in charge of supplying the tournament sites with shirts reviewed sales figures from the year before and the site manager's comments. The reports came back with comments like, "We could have sold 200 more t-shirts and 100 more sweatshirts." During telephone calls to verify that information, the same managers stated that estimates on the report were low.

Based on that information, hundreds of additional shirts were printed and shipped to the tournament sites. At the end of the tournament, only a fraction of those *hundreds* of shirts were actually purchased, creating heavy losses for the shirt vendor.

The moral of this story is that hard facts work better than an off-the-cuff review of a situation. Base your promotions on actual statistics!

Gathering Information From External Sources

You can reference a variety of external sources to help you plan your promotions. Some magazines related to the athletic business world, such as *Athletic Business* and *Scholastic Coach*, reference companies that can provide you with sources for promotional items or programs. You can also subscribe to a number of sport and event marketing newsletters (warning—they are pricey!) or find them at larger libraries.

Frequently, nothing works better than speaking with a professional in the business to ask about tricks of the trade. A local college or university may have a promotion specialist on its athletic staff. If a stadium or arena of medium to large size exists in your area, or if a professional sport team of any level is nearby, its marketing pros might be able to spend a few minutes with you to describe how things can work at your level. A benefit to those contacts is that they will know the local environment (as opposed to the global terms discussed here), and can be very specific in the directions they can point you. It is unlikely that these marketing people will perceive you as competition. In fact, you might come up with a promotion between that minor league professional team and your community, creating a win-win situation.

Some state high school athletic or activities associations provide reference materials to their members. An excellent example is the Illinois High School Association's Pack the Place promotion, a winter, regular-season statewide promotion program which has a proven track record of increasing attendance. To maintain this information for future reference, the day planner idea presented previously becomes a possibility, and many computer software programs are also now available. You can create forms and keep records that are easily referenced.

When investigating a planning system, you should look for flexibility. Hard-copy day planners with forms that fit into a three-ring (or more) binder, offer simple to highly detailed forms. You can find many of these forms at a local office supply superstore. Computer software will let you develop your own forms from scratch or provide sample forms you can modify to meet your needs. If you have the knowledge and patience, you can use some of the more advanced word processing and desktop publishing programs to create custom forms.

Examples of such programs available include Microsoft Word and WordPerfect. Both have standard forms you can modify to meet your needs and the ability to let you create your own forms. Software packages like Microsoft Works combine word processing, database, and other functions you can utilize in your daily tasks.

INVOLVING KEY MEMBERS OF THE ORGANIZATION

No matter what kind of promotion program you want to develop, it's difficult to do it alone. We are going to look at different ways you can involve individuals and groups, from inside and outside your organization, to assist you in executing promotions. Form 3.2 can be easily attached to your checklists and forms, providing the roster of people who will work with each promotion.

Involving Appropriate Individuals and Groups

First, you may be able to identify an individual in your organization who would like to work in the promotion area as an avocation. This person might be a teacher or support staff member with some gift for great promotion ideas and the people skills to get different individuals together to work toward a common goal. You might find one person with expertise in printing and another in fund-raising. These are people who will take the checklists and run with them, but know that the director has the final say in everything. They will relieve you of a lot of busy work.

Student Help

Students may also perform some of these tasks, distributing posters and other promotional materials, and writing copy for programs and other printed promotions. You might also assign students to work with adults to whom you have delegated the authority to execute certain projects.

Other school groups, such as a business or graphics class, are also possibilities. Taking on certain promotional responsibilities in a supervised setting can provide students with a great hands-on learning experience. This concept will be discussed further in print promotions in chapter 5.

Booster Clubs

One of your most essential organized groups outside the school building is the booster club. A well-organized booster club can become your promotion vehicle, providing some of the following services:

1. Soliciting advertising for programs and sponsors
2. Working behind the scenes to develop promotions and fund-raisers
3. Assisting with the production of printed promotions
4. Serving in hands-on roles at events where promotions are being staged

▮ Form 3.2 Individual/Support Group Involvement

This form will help you detail the assistance you could receive from student and adult support groups. Fill in the blanks below as necessary. The meeting notes by date are a good way to keep a time line for your discussions with this group.

Sport: ______________________________

Level: ______________________________

Date: ______________________________

Name of individual or group: ______________________________

____

Area of support: ______________________________

Venue and capacity: ______________________________

Key telephone numbers: ______________________________

____

____

____

Responsibilities and due dates: ______________________________

____

____

____

Meeting notes

Date	Items discussed
________	______________________________
________	______________________________
________	______________________________
________	______________________________
________	______________________________
________	______________________________
________	______________________________

Every organization's booster club is structured differently, but three patterns seem to prevail:

1. Your school has an umbrella booster club that supports the entire sport program (most desirable).
2. Your school has separate booster clubs for each sport or activity, but key individuals from each sport club form a board to coordinate the activities and prevent each other from stepping on toes (also desirable).
3. Your school has separate booster clubs by sport, which literally compete with each other (undesirable).

The first two types are what every sport director hopes to work with. Homogeneous groups tend to have more people who work year after year with the booster club, as opposed to individuals who take part only when their youngsters are participating. You may find that members of the booster club expand the range of talents assisting you through their own diverse experiences.

The extent to which you involve booster clubs will vary according to your community. You have to measure the effectiveness of the group, judge its personalities, and discover whether the club as a whole or certain members of the club have expectations they want filled in return for their involvement. Politics can come in, and you have to decide whether you want to play that game and by whose rules it will be played.

A Booster Club Contract

Horror stories abound, relating how influential members of a school's athletic booster club have put pressure on a sport director and school administrators over the hiring and firing of coaches. One school in western Michigan put a stop to that—at least in its community.

Faced with dependence on its booster club for funding, Tri-County High School in Howard City, Michigan, entered an agreement with the booster club regarding its role in the school sport program. The agreement made it clear that the efforts of the booster club to raise money are appreciated. However, it also stated in no uncertain terms that the decision-making process was in the hands of the school administration. The party controlling the purse strings did not control the athletic department.

Sharing Responsibilities

A well-developed promotion, perhaps for a major event, integrates all the elements that will be discussed in this book's final five chapters. If you plan to involve key members from different groups of the organization, you will have to go back to the checklists and forms discussed earlier and add a form, which is a responsibility tree for that project. Figure 3.2 is a sample responsibility tree that you may adapt and attach to Form 3.2. The responsibility tree is like an organizational chart with the athletic director at the top. From there, general responsibilities described in Form 3.2 are delegated to specific groups.

You have ultimate responsibility in this process. However, the final responsibility tree may be developed by the individual or group delegated the responsibility for that promotion. You need to communicate closely with the first party beneath you on the responsibility tree to ensure the successful execution of a promotion.

A key is to avoid responsibility overlap among key individuals and groups. Don't involve two different groups in a common responsibility (i.e., print). However, make sure these individuals and groups meet on a regular schedule in advance of the promotion or report back to you periodically to maintain information flow and avoid surprises.

Gaining Commitment

If you want to get a group committed to working on promotion, you need to follow a few principles after you sit down and make the pitch for them to get involved.

- Don't overwork them.
- Give them a very specific direction.
- Give them recognition.

Anyone can sit down and talk anybody into doing just about anything. Keeping them happy while they do it is much more difficult.

Again, your checklists need to include an activity report for each group and individual assisting you in your promotion program. Although this may seem like a lot of work, think of the public relations problems you could have once you get one key individual or group against you. Activity reports help you reduce the likelihood of these conflicts arising.

Some groups may be large enough that you can involve different individuals for different promotions.

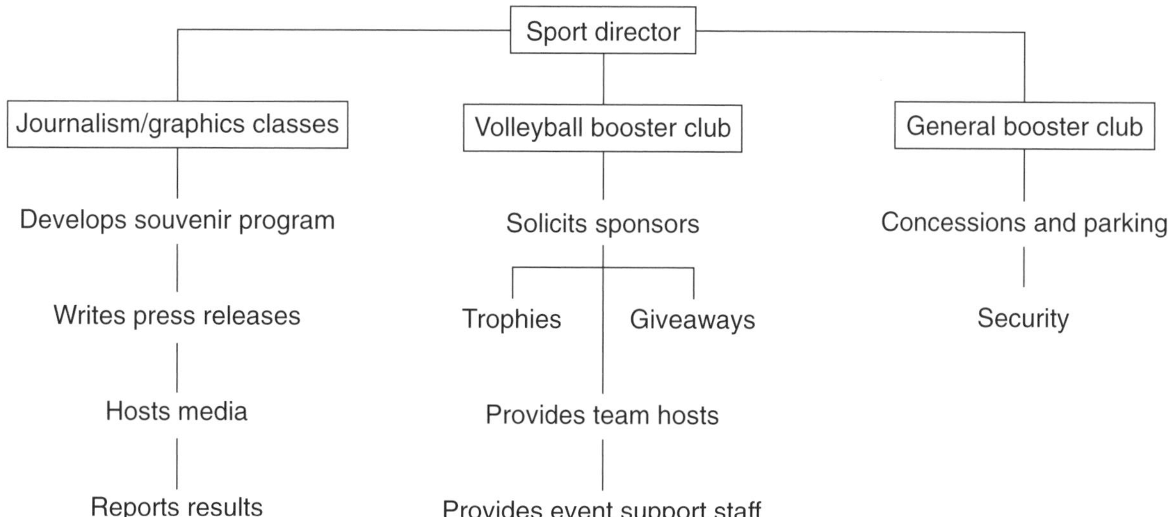

Figure 3.2 Sample responsibility tree.

Booster clubs are good examples. Booster clubs that have a common reporting and organizing mechanism will not involve a lot of the same people from sport to sport unless those adults are somehow related to an athlete who participates in two or more sports. Booster clubs are advantageous to promotion by bringing together people as a group who are willing to support your program. The absence of such a group would require that you contact people individually to solicit support for different tasks.

PLANNING FOR EVALUATION

No promotion is complete without a thorough evaluation involving all parties who took part in its execution. Don't say a promotion was successful simply because you saw the stands full and sponsors are happy.

Mechanisms for evaluating promotions vary by type of promotion. For example, if you were staging a special night with giveaways and contests, you might use some of the following criteria:

- Attendance
- Number of giveaway items distributed
- Number of mentions for sponsor (public address, program, other)
- Student involvement
- Costs
- Personnel (i.e., hours in preparation)

A fund-raiser would use different evaluation criteria than would a print promotion. Form 3.3 provides a general idea for evaluating basic promotions. To evaluate impact, you may want to compare game promotions to previous years when a promotion did not take place for the same event. This can be a tricky example though, because win-loss records can come into play. Be sure to include that intangible in your criteria.

You should also evaluate the timetable used to execute each promotion and make adjustments on your master calendar as necessary. Also examine the hours put in by individuals assigned to the project and whether individuals and groups fulfilled their responsibilities.

Evaluate and write notes as each promotion is executed and immediately following the promotion. Provide your overall critique immediately, and if changes need to be made, make them in an expedient, professional manner during the days and weeks afterward. Never wait until you are at the initial stages of a similar promotion the following year to tell people they are not involved or are reassigned to a greater or lesser task because of something that happened the year before.

Form 3.3 Evaluating a Promotion

After staging a promotion activity, use this form to evaluate each area within the promotion. For example, if a certain promotion involved print and public relations, use a separate form for each.

Sport: ______________________________

Level: ______________________________

Date: ______________________________

Type of promotion(s): ______________________________

____

____

Area of evaluation: ______________________________

Objectives: ______________________________

____

____

Results: ______________________________

____

____

____

Positives: ______________________________

____

____

Challenges: ______________________________

____

____

Adjust for next year's promotion: ______________________________

____

____

Support individual/group involvement evaluation: ______________________________

____

____

____

Summary

To develop a promotion plan,

1. recognize the need for intricate planning of each promotion;
2. develop a record-keeping system for each promotion;
3. collect resources to assist you in developing a promotion plan;
4. involve people within and outside the organization in the promotion plan, and keep those individuals committed and happy; and
5. evaluate promotions completely.

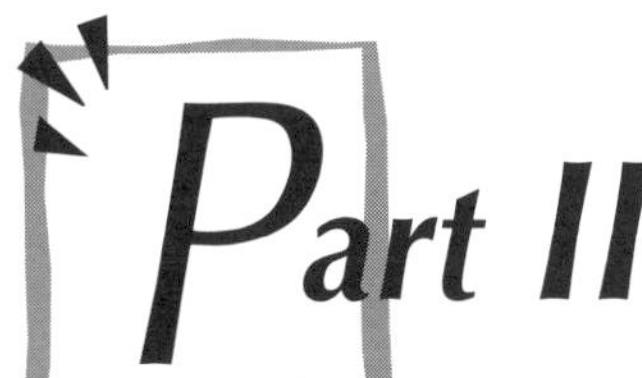

Part II

Implementing and Evaluating the Promotion Plan

Chapter 4

Building Positive Public Relations

Your ability to implement an effective promotion program hinges on your program or organization having a positive public image. In fact, if the horse and cart theory were applied here, the strong horse of a positive public image really pulls the promotion cart. People in your school and community will rally around a program that everyone feels good about. This support will persist at a high level even when the win-loss scale doesn't tip in your favor.

To be successful, a public relations campaign should be inclusive of all of your school's co-curricular programs—athletic and nonathletic. Often the two groups are polarized, especially since athletic teams tend to receive more attention in the public eye than, for example, music and drama.

If the elements of your public relations program are inclusive, others' perceptions of the school program as a whole will improve, cooperative relationships between co-curricular groups will develop, and the overall marketability of your program will be enhanced.

Building that positive image involves effort more than anything else. You can throw a little money at it if you want, but public relations, media relations, and publicity are all within your control. They aren't things you get a corporate sponsor for, but they will attract corporate sponsors.

In this chapter, you will learn

1. how a positive external public relations image begins with positive public relations within your school or organization,
2. how to reach out into the community with a positive public relations program,
3. how to understand and work with your local media,
4. how to involve your personnel in your image program,
5. how to obtain free publicity for your program, and
6. how to evaluate your public relations efforts.

UNDERSTANDING PUBLIC RELATIONS

Some believe the term *public relations* automatically incorporates your publicity and media relations efforts as well. While in a global sense the three work well together, each is unique.

Public relations is just that: interacting with the various publics within your organization and your community to deliver your message. Public relations is not as easy as publicity, because instead of taking advantage of opportunities to promote your program without a lot of interaction, working with people brings unique variables to the table. Public relations also differs from media relations: The media is used to *deliver* your message to your final audience, the public.

MANAGING PUBLIC RELATIONS WITHIN THE SCHOOL OR ORGANIZATION

The image-building of a public relations program begins within your school. Working within your own system is the first stepping stone to creating opportunities to deliver a positive message about your program. This point is critical because if the organization is to end up with its best foot forward as the external public relations campaign begins, your internal people need to feel good about it. The principle is similar to a sales manager getting representatives to adopt the same sales pitch for a product. You can use a variety of ideas to get your entire sales force on the same page.

More Than Athletics

The sport program often becomes a target for nonsport people because it tends to attract the most attention of all co-curricular activities. As we discussed in earlier chapters about philosophy, having as many student activity groups as possible form an alliance becomes a great selling point. Involvement of groups, such as National Honor Society, music, and others, in support roles for the athletic program creates more cooperation than competition, and underscores that all co-curricular activities benefit the students, the school, and the community. Selling a total program, rather than just a sport program, may encourage the community and corporate sponsors to consider supporting a wider variety of activities at your school.

The Preseason Meeting

One of the most positive public relations programs you can launch is the preseason meeting. In this forum, you can mandate the attendance of your athletes and their parents, and take that opportunity to have the program sell itself. See Figure 4.1 for a sample preseason meeting schedule.

Some school districts publicize these meetings to the general public, sometimes under a "Meet the Team" banner, but the primary purpose is to get participants and their families to this meeting. In addition to familiarizing yourself with the athletes, parents, and possibly other fans, this meeting becomes a great opportunity for this group to put your face, and your coaches' faces, with names. It's also a great time to explain some of the athletic policies of your school and state athletic association pertaining to eligibility and team membership (some state associations have brochures on eligibility that they encourage schools to distribute to parents). If nothing else, you head off some potential problems by getting them to understand how your program operates.

An important note here is that a good public relations person wants everyone to be happy with the company line, but what's even more important is that the company line is understood. At times, certain policies (i.e., breaking team training rules) come under community criticism when they have to be enforced. Often, parents of the students involved are not made aware of the policies until the rules infraction occurs.

By explaining policies in a preseason meeting with participants' parents present, those parents become potential ambassadors for you rather than adversaries. A sheet of paper sent home with a student sometimes doesn't make it into the parent's hands. The preseason meeting becomes a great preventative measure in this respect.

Preseason Meeting Schedule
Your High School Gymnasium
August 15, 199__

7:00 p.m.	Welcome, comments from Principal Jones
7:05 p.m.	Comments from Athletic Director Baer, preview of upcoming evening • Explanation of eligibility brochure • Explanation of team rules • Explanation of school media policies • Sportsmanship discussion • Introduction of coaching staff
7:30 p.m.	Comments from head coaches about upcoming seasons
7:45 p.m.	Demonstration of rule changes by team members and officials from Greater Oaks Official's Association
8:15 p.m.	Individual sports meetings in assigned rooms
8:45 p.m.	Reception—soft drinks, coffee, and cookies

Figure 4.1 Preseason meeting schedule.

In addition to describing policies, you can take time to emphasize the value of the program to the students, parents, and community; what the school is doing to promote those values; and how parents and other fans can support that effort.

If the meeting is for a specific sport, this forum gives your coaching staff an excellent opportunity to demonstrate some of the strategies the team will pursue during the season, and local game officials can be invited to speak about the rules of the game and some of the important rule changes for the upcoming season. Players and coaches should be available to demonstrate certain situations so officials can explain what constitutes the proper call (i.e., a block versus a charge in basketball).

Similar to understanding policy, that parent who has had a game strategy or basis for an official's call explained in a preseason meeting is an ambassador for your program, becoming a likely candidate to explain to other spectators during games what is really taking place. It may also cut down on the number of times a parent contacts you or a coach to ask questions or express concerns about the program.

If the meeting is an all-sports meeting for that season, sometimes the individual sports break out for their own meetings in different parts of the building after the general meeting is concluded. Other groups, like the marching band, can also get exposure through these meetings. It is simply a matter of having a philosophy that incorporates as many people as possible into the sport program and adjusting your preseason meeting format to include them.

The Homeroom Presentation

If your school allows, conducting a preseason meeting for the entire student body during homeroom time, a class, or an all-school assembly can be effective. Determining the most effective forum for your school really depends heavily on size. Running a preseason meeting for 1,000 students at one time is not likely to work well—holding the attention of that many young people is difficult.

The amount of time spent in an all-student setting should be considerably less than that spent with athletes and their parents. School administrators may be reluctant to give up class time or homeroom time to have a coach or single-sport team talk about its upcoming season.

In-room presentations are most effective when they combine the efforts of administration, coaches, teachers, and students. A homeroom presentation made by administrators can help students realize the topic is important.

Figure 4.2 describes sample formats for two brief homeroom presentations, one involving classroom appearances by individuals, the other involving the school-wide presentation of a brief videotape to help

Homeroom Sportsmanship Presentation
In-Room Presentation

Purpose of the presentation

The purpose is to make students aware of these factors:

- There is a need for exemplary behavior at school sporting events—different than that exhibited at college and professional games.
- This goal is shared by the superintendent, board of education, teachers, parents, and many students.
- After-school programs are an extension of the regular school day, with all school rules and regulations in effect.

Who makes the presentation

- A high-level administrator at the school. Students are accustomed to hearing about sports and sportsmanship from coaches. Having a high-level administrator make the presentation will attach a greater sense of importance.
- A top student-athlete. Peer pressure from a respected member of the student body also gets the message across.

The tone of the presentation

- Talk about respect and treating others the way you want to be treated.
- Discuss why sportsmanship is an important aspect of educational athletics and part of the learning process.
- Focus on the positives of good sportsmanship rather than on the negative consequences of unsportsmanlike behavior.

What is generally expected of students

- Demonstrate positive enthusiasm without causing harm, danger, or embarrassment to others or to the school.
- Follow all rules at after-school events that are in effect during the school day.
- Demonstrate respect toward fellow students, opponents, players, coaches, and officials.
- Demand proper behavior from fellow students. An individual's behavior can affect the whole group.
- Demonstrate respect and pride for the school.

What is specifically expected of students

- Respect opponents. Respect is the key to good sportsmanship. Opponents are not enemies but fellow teenagers who happen to attend other schools.
- Be modest and humble in victory or defeat. Be a gracious winner and show class when you lose.

(continued)

Figure 4.2 Homeroom sportsmanship presentation.

- Acknowledge good plays by both teams.
- Show concern for anyone who is injured. Give concerned applause when an injured athlete is aided from the field.
- Work together with cheerleaders on positive cheers. Avoid obscene, degrading, or elitist cheers—when you participate in an elitist cheer, you support an elitist image.
- After the game, do not tease or belittle the opponent in any way. Be pleasant and gracious to everyone.

Video Presentation

If your school delivers daily announcements via video on an in-house system, consider producing or obtaining a short tape (no more than 5 to 10 minutes) that discusses the need for sportsmanship.

The tape can deliver some of the same messages in a format similar to the in-room presentation. The tape could also include action footage from games, which is more likely to hold the attention of the students.

Some leagues (the Twin Valley Conference in southern Michigan, for example) have produced a video involving students and administrators from each school talking about sportsmanship. Making this kind of tape could be an excellent project for a video class or club.

Figure 4.2 *(continued)*

enlist the participation and support of other students for your program.

Selling Sportsmanship in the Classroom

Grosse Pointe North High School in suburban Detroit developed its homeroom presentation concept in the late 1980s, when it was having sportsmanship problems at its events. Different administrators and coaches delivered a message regarding expected behavior at an athletic event on campus or at another school, and what the consequences were for those students who did not live up to those standards.

"We just assumed that everybody knew what was good sportsmanship and what was expected of them when they attended an athletic event," said North athletic director Tom Gauerke. "We made a bad assumption."

Sending Letters Home

Sending something in writing to the parents of your athletes or the parents of every member of your student body is another method of reaching out within your school community. The letter need not be long. It can cover athletic department policies or the value of co-curricular activities in the development of a student, or target a specific event. It is a good idea to start with something that encourages student participation and adult support. It can also stress the lifelong values taught in your program, as shown in Figure 4.3.

These letters can be distributed in a scheduled district-wide mailing or be sent home with students. Cost considerations impact the former option, and the possibility of a hand-delivered letter not making it to the intended recipient affects the latter, but this communication method still has potential.

Running Columns in School Building Newsletters

Some schools publish monthly or quarterly newsletters that are sent home with students. Sport directors also get an occasional opportunity to communicate with all of the taxpayers in a school district through a periodic newsletter. Space devoted to athletics becomes an excellent venue to combine any of the ideas presented in team meetings, homeroom presentations, and letters home.

Dear Parent:

Your role in the education of a youngster is important. Support shown in the home is often manifested in the ability of the student to accept the opportunities presented at school in the classroom and through co-curricular activities.

There is a value system—established in the home, nurtured in the school—that young people are developing. Their involvement in classroom and other activities contributes to that development. Integrity, fairness, and respect are lifetime values taught through athletics, and these are the principles of good sportsmanship. With them, the spirit of competition thrives, fueled by honest rivalry, courteous relations, and graceful acceptance of the results.

A good sport, whether a student or a parent, is a true leader in the community. As a parent of a student at our school, your sportsmanship goals should include

- realizing that athletics are part of the educational experience, and the benefits of involvement go beyond the final score of a game;
- encouraging our students to perform their best, just as we would urge them on with their classwork, knowing that others will always turn in better or lesser performances;
- participating in positive cheers that encourage our youngsters, and discouraging any cheers that would redirect that focus;
- learning, understanding, and respecting the rules of the game, the officials who administer them, and their decisions;
- respecting the task our coaches face as teachers, and supporting them as they strive to educate our youth;
- respecting our opponents as students, and acknowledging them for striving to do their best;
- developing a sense of dignity under all circumstances; and
- being a fan—not a fanatic!

These and other expectations are included in the attached guidelines, which we hope you will take a few moments to review. They give us a road map to follow toward a more educational atmosphere for interscholastic athletics.

You can have a major influence on your youngster's attitude about academics and athletics. The leadership role you take in sportsmanship will help influence your child and our community for years to come.

We look forward to serving you in the year ahead and appreciate your continued support.

Sincerely,

Athletic Director

(continued)

Figure 4.3 Letter to parents.

Fair Play Among the Spectators

- Remember that you are at a contest to support and yell for your team and to enjoy the skill and competition, but you are not to intimidate or ridicule the other team and its fans.
- Remember that school athletes are students and that they sometimes make mistakes. Praise student-athletes for their attempts to improve, just as you would praise students working in the classroom.
- Remember that holding a ticket to a school athletic event is a privilege to observe the contest, not a license to assault others verbally or to be otherwise obnoxious.
- Learn the rules of the game to understand and appreciate certain situations that take place during a contest.
- Show respect for opposing players, coaches, spectators, and support groups. Treat them as you would treat a guest in your home.
- Never taunt or insult opponents during the game. Avoid comments of an ethnic, racial, or sexual nature.
- Respect the integrity and judgment of game officials. They do their best to promote student-athletes, so admire their willingness to participate in full view of the public!
- Show appreciation for an outstanding play by either team.
- Refrain from using alcohol or drugs before, during, and after games on or near the site of the event (i.e., no tailgating).
- Cheer only in a way that supports and uplifts the teams involved.
- Compliment school and league administrators for their efforts to support educational athletics and fair play.
- Be a positive model through your own actions and censure poor behavior in other spectators.

Figure 4.3 *(continued)*

Using School Media

School media still tend to be as strong a source of positive exposure for your program as they were 25 years ago. Young sport reporters seek to please everyone with their stories as they begin to struggle with their objectivity toward a situation.

We've elected to keep school media separate from traditional media. You don't *own* them, but your school paper and student radio and television outlets may offer opportunities to have a story told or get a message out that would not be available in community media outlets.

You could also encourage a writer to address selected issues in your building, such as team eligibility, training rules, or sportsmanship, and ask that space be allotted on a regular basis for the sport director or a coach to communicate with the student body. You could also provide additional story ideas. Remember that the bottom line for student media is cuddle, but don't censor!

Creating a School Speakers Bureau

Many professional sport teams and organizations have developed speakers bureaus to reach out to different parts of the community. You can use this same concept on a limited basis within your school as a great public relations tool.

Your coaches and well-spoken players in any sport can talk to middle school and elementary school kids in your system. Varsity athletes are often the first heroes an elementary school student has, and their position gains instant respect at that level. Youngsters see a varsity athlete walk in the room, especially wearing a game jersey, and they are in awe. Speech topics can range from the team outlook for the season, to game rules and sportsmanship, and from drug and alcohol abuse to peer pressure.

As the sport director, you will need to make arrangements with the elementary and junior high/ middle school administration to set up such appearances by your coaches and athletes. You must also ensure that these visits are not interpreted as recruiting efforts by your high school. Check your state athletic association guidelines on this matter.

You probably have a general idea about which coaches would make good representatives in a speakers bureau, but seek coaches' advice to identify potential candidates among your athletes. Don't assume that the senior point guard on a basketball team is a great public speaker just because she has been elected a team captain. Speaking roles on the playing field and in the classroom differ dramatically.

If your school system offers classes in speech, or has programs such as debate or forensics, encourage athletes to participate in them early in their high school careers. First, it will help them develop the communication skills that will make them more effective leaders on their teams; and second, these speaking skills will become that much more valuable to them as they advance to college and the working world. Of course, it will also help you identify potential members of your speakers bureau.

You should work with coaches and athletes to develop the messages that will be delivered through the speakers bureau. You should have students practice presentations and evaluate them before they are presented in a classroom setting.

REACHING OUT TO THE COMMUNITY

As you move outside your school into the community at large, two major public relations avenues can help you interact with the other people with whom you live and work.

Speakers Bureau II

This speakers bureau primarily involves you and head coaches, going out in the community to talk with groups on a regular basis. Rotary, Kiwanis, or local Y meetings provide excellent opportunities for you and your staff to be visible in the community.

Topics need not always be specifically on a team. You can use such stages to talk about the benefits of co-curricular athletics for kids. Coaches might talk about trends they see within their respective sports, leaving the door open to come back at another time to talk about their teams. These presentations need to be structured to allow for a question and answer period that will help promote the interaction you want between your program and the community.

The very best speakers among your athletes can also get involved. Speaking to a civic group is a wonderful opportunity for a young person, and it helps put some of the best products of our educational system on display. The talk by the student need not, and should not, be lengthy, only enough to provide a positive experience for all parties involved.

The subject matter for your athletes in this setting will differ somewhat from the presentations made to elementary and junior high/middle school students. Potential topics include the educational role of participation in co-curricular activities (not just athletics if possible) and talking about sportsmanship and other athletic program issues.

Involvement in Community Drives

Making your sport program visible in community activities beyond the playing field can generate some of the best public relations. This element of public relations can involve you, your coaching staff, and your athletes.

Participating in a food collection or blood drive (perhaps with a contest between teams) or a variety of charitable or civic programs creates a warm feeling about your sport program, while providing your coaches and players with a character-building experience. Not only can that intangible come back to boost your program's image, but it could also pay dividends at the gate on game nights. Participation in civic events, such as a local festival, where a team helps provide a service like running a food concession or some kind of a game, can also turn into a fund-raising activity for that team or the school.

Ensure that all from your program who participate in such endeavors wear a game jersey or something that identifies them as being part of the team. The presence of uniforms sometimes creates a photo opportunity for local newspapers or television stations.

UNDERSTANDING AND WORKING WITH THE MEDIA

"You saw some scores missing from tonight's scoreboard, so we remind you to call us here at TV-6 as soon as your game is over."

"The Trojans were out to a 35 to 0 lead, but we can't report the final score because nobody called us."

"I'm sorry, Mrs. Jones, but if the school doesn't call us with the information, we can't print it in the paper."

These statements have been used innumerable times on the air and over the telephone by reporters, television sportscasters, and newspaper sports editors when they couldn't relay information about teams from their area to their respective audiences because schools failed to fulfill their responsibility in the media relations process. Getting the word out about your different teams through the media is an ongoing process. Like running a play or perfecting a skill, it requires a lot of work. And like scoring a touchdown or winning the race, the hard work is rewarded.

How Media Coverage Works

Times were when certain schools or teams received automatic media coverage. These days, with so many sporting events for the media to cover, and available space disproportionate to the number of events taking place, it behooves you and your coaches to make sure you take every step to ensure results, schedules, and features about your teams appear in the media.

Some local newspapers may have 20 to 30 schools in their coverage area, some regional newspapers many more than twice that number. Even so, on a given day, one school winning three conference titles may dominate the sports page. The media outlet is not biased if it provides information about winners. And, if a school is on the fringe of the outlet's coverage area, where the outlet isn't receiving much advertising or selling many papers, the attention received is often minimal. If you want publicity through the media for your school, you must set up a program to make sure it happens. It's your responsibility, not the media's!

Media Relations Before the Season Begins

Before the teams even begin practices, the media needs information about them. Like you or the coach, media outlets need to plan their event coverage weeks in advance. Depending on the size of the media markets your school is part of, your personal visit in advance of the school year can pay great dividends during the months that follow, and it doesn't hurt to follow up by phone or mail before winter and spring seasons.

Though perceived as public entities, newspapers, cable systems, and radio and television stations are businesses with one primary function: to make money. They face no obligation—no matter how large or small the community—to make the coverage of your sports teams a priority. At the same time most media outlets thrive on local information to report.

The Who-What-When Formula

To work with journalists, you have to think like one. The basic formula to getting publicity is a journalistic formula: You need to find out about who, what, and when, ideally during a preseason meeting with the community's sport directors and editors.

Who

When you meet with the sports editor or director at your local newspaper, television, or radio station, try to obtain the names of the different staff members. Hopefully, you'll get to meet some of them during your visit. Remember that on nights of events, your coaches or other individuals delegated the responsibility for making the call won't always deal with the head of the sports department. In fact, many newspapers traditionally use part-time personnel (referred to as *stringers*) to take calls and write game summaries.

The *Whos* you meet have various responsibilities, including

- the sports editor,
- the prep writer,
- other full-time staff members, and
- part-time writers or stringers.

At some papers, one person may be designated the primary or *beat* writer for prep sports. That person, instead of the sports editor or director, may be your daily contact.

What

Find out exactly what your local media outlets want to receive from you or your coaches when calling in results. Some newspapers even provide forms for you to work from when calling.

Often, people answering the phone at a television or radio station only want

- the score and
- a unique fact about the game.

The unique fact could be that the winning team is still undefeated or won the league title. It could be that a certain player scored 30 points or rushed for four touchdowns. Individuals responsible for calling the media may or may not find an opportunity to pass on that information. They should not get discouraged if all the outlet wants is the score. Remember, a TV station often has only about 4 minutes or less to report on all the games in your area.

Newspapers generally ask for the following after getting the final score:

- Score by quarters, periods, or innings
- A scoring summary of the game
- A key play
- Other key statistics

Newspapers and radio stations in some communities prefer that the coach always make the call following the game to provide quotes to use in print or on the air.

When

When is the most critical of the three *W*s. Your school must provide information within the media deadlines. Remember that the deadline is the end of the calling period. If a call is made on deadline, the chances of having the game reported in a manner similar to those who called well in advance of the deadline diminish, a relevant point for information called in prior to games, as well as after them.

Many newspapers publish a special mid-week prep section in which nominations for standout performances or statistics are sought. Calling in just before the deadline actually decreases your chances of being included. Being one of the first callers is preferable to being one of the last. The bottom line is that how the media represents your school depends on whether you provide the proper information in a timely manner.

This approach works for small schools on the fringe of a circulation area or TV-radio signal, as well as large schools that have traditionally been covered heavily. Fulfilling the three *W*s builds a strong rapport with the media and pays dividends, regardless of the kind of season you are having.

Failing to fulfill the three *W*s will backfire. The media keep track of schools, sport directors, and coaches who call only when they win, call late, or provide incomplete or inaccurate information (such as making up the names of opposing players). Media outlets often choose not to report those winning results if that's the only time they receive information about a team.

Preseason Information

Two items every media outlet needs before the season begins are copies of your team schedule and complete rosters. Schedules take priority, assisting outlets in their coverage planning. A complete schedule lists the games in sequential order with the date, day of the week, name of the opponent, site, and game time, as shown in the sample schedule in Figure 4.4. Also designate which games are home games, and if some events are staged at neutral sites (like a league meet), or if home games are played at an off-campus site, include it as well.

Send team rosters to the media before the first contest so they can be kept on file. You cannot assume that reporters and camera operators will receive programs when they arrive at your games. Some newspapers key information they receive from the schools in their coverage area into their computers. When a school calls in a result, the stringer or other staff member taking the information calls up the roster on the computer, knowing that the names will match the roster the school sent in during the preseason. Don't presume that an opponent calling in the results will have the correct names and numbers of your players.

The media appreciate receiving numerical rosters, such as the one shown in Figure 4.5, ranked in order from the lowest to the highest number. Amazingly,

Your High School
199_ Varsity Football Schedule

Date	Opponent/site	Time
Sept. 1	at Millersburg	7:00 p.m.
Sept. 8	WACHOVIA*	7:30 p.m.
Sept. 15	GAS CITY*	7:30 p.m.
Sept. 22	at Bloomington*	8:00 p.m.
Sept. 29	at Monroeville	8:00 p.m.
Oct. 5	BUGGSVILLE* (Homecoming)	7:30 p.m.
Oct. 12	Bakersfield Central (at Mountain Dome)	8:00 p.m.
Oct. 19	MOUNT FORESTER*	7:30 p.m.
Oct. 26	BELLEVILLE* (Parent's Night)	7:30 p.m.

Home games in CAPITALS. All home games played at Murphy Field.
*Denotes Northwestern Conference games

Figure 4.4 Sample schedule.

Your High School
Boys Basketball Roster

No.	Name	Pos.	Ht.	Wt.	Class
10	Bradley Charles*	G	6-0	175	Jr.
12	Todd Angevine*	F	6-2	185	Sr.
14	Mike Gallihugh**	G	5-11	160	Sr.
20	Kevin Milan	G	5-9	165	Jr.
22	Joe Simons	F	6-3	195	Jr.
24	Steve Kirsch**	G-F	6-1	190	Sr.
30	Steve Van Dam	F	6-2	200	So.
32	Winston Plymouth	F	6-3	200	Jr.
34	Joe Johnson	G	5-11	190	So.
40	Aaron Baer	C	6-5	210	Jr.
42	Gary Williams	F	6-4	200	So.
44	Bob Thomas	C-F	6-5	220	Sr.

Head coach: Robert Montgomery
Assistant coaches: Royce Dakich, Walt Felling, Kit Newburgh
Managers: Mike Fox, Mike Wowo, Eric Rudeman
Trainer: Doc Williams
Cheerleaders: Erin Rebecca, Cari Angevine, Michelle Gallihugh, Heather Howe, Judy Panetta, Jan Boone

*indicates one letter won
**indicates two letters won

Figure 4.5 Sample roster.

a number of high school rosters list players alphabetically, by class, or randomly. Reporters and photographers will not always know your players by name, and referencing a numerical list is the quickest way to determine who's who. The roster should also include first and last names of players, avoiding nicknames whenever possible. Height, weight, and number of varsity letters won by the athletes also helps.

MEETING WITH YOUR COACHES ABOUT THE MEDIA

Once you have determined the needs of the different media outlets, communicate that information to your coaches or the individuals responsible for calling in the information.

Prepare a call-in sheet, similar to the one shown in Figure 4.6, with telephone numbers, contact names, and deadlines for each media outlet, then provide this information to the responsible party in each sport. Ideally, you should prepare this form in a format that can be attached to the inside cover of a scorebook or other statistics keeping book. Review the proper procedures with each party responsible for calling in results, stressing accuracy and calling immediately after the conclusion of a game.

If the person calling in the results is not a coach, let the media outlets know that, either with a phone call or a note to the sports editor, director, or prep coordinator at each outlet in advance of the season. Some newspapers have a policy of not accepting results from anyone other than the coach, especially not taking calls from parents. You may want to include a note on your telephone list if a media outlet will only take calls from the coach or you.

REPORTING RESULTS

Regardless of where a contest takes place, it is the school's responsibility to call in results unless you, the coach, or a designated caller is certain that members of the local media attended the entire event or other advance arrangements have been made. Some leagues covered by common media have a long-standing practice of having the home team call.

Your High School
Postgame Calls

Call immediately after event. Keep trying until you reach them.

Daily Tribune 555-555-5555 Collect from New Castle High Football if on the road

Wants scoring summary and statistics, other details
Deadline is midnight on weekends, 11 p.m. on weeknights, and 8 a.m. the following morning. You can fax report form to 555-777-7777 and then call number above to confirm receipt of fax.

Times-Herald 555-555-9999 Collect if on the road

Wants scoring summary and statistics, other details
Deadline is 1 a.m. every night. Fax report form to 555-888-8888.

WBWB Radio 555-555-2222 Collect if on the road

Will want score and a couple of highlights
Will use score when they get it. Details are for morning sports at 6:15 a.m. and 7:15 a.m.

WTTV-TV 555-555-3333 Collect if on the road

Ask for Chuck Fisher or Don Marlowe. Will want score and outstanding scorers.
Need by 10:45 p.m. for 11 p.m. sports.

Figure 4.6 Postgame call-in sheet.

If you know that a writer from the local paper was present, and the local radio station broadcast the game, you need not make those calls. However, at times newspapers or television stations send camera operators to get snapshots or some video of the game. Those people are not sent to get the score or many details, and they often move from game to game.

If your school plays a contest on the road, you might make advance arrangements with the opponent for calling in the final score and statistics. If there is ever a doubt about who should call after the game, make sure your school calls in the results. Even if the other school already called, the outlet may wish to obtain additional information and will appreciate that your school took the time to ensure they got the report.

Timeliness

You can generally make collect calls from away contests. These calls should be made immediately after the game, from the game site. Time on road games is critical. As previously mentioned, the sooner you call, allowing the most lead time possible before the outlet's deadline, the greater your chances of receiving coverage.

Make the Call Before You Get Called!

Two favorite stories illustrate the importance of reporting results on time. The first involves a sports editor who woke a school superintendent well past midnight because a sport director failed to see that the coach phoned in the results of a football game. In the second incident, the local wire service tracked down an individual responsible for calling in the results of a state track meet, well after the fact, in a local watering hole.

Who-What-When Reports

The three *W*s we discussed earlier should be your guide when calling in results. For those outlets that want more information than the final score, the three Ws translate to *who* did . . . *what* . . . *when*.

As critical as making the call and making it on time is providing accurate information. The more complete and accurate the information you provide, the easier you have made their job and the better your chance of receiving coverage.

You will need rosters for both teams. If calling in a wrestling, track, or swimming and diving invitational result, you need full names for all individuals whose results you'll report. Statistics for both teams is also a key. We could fill another book with the importance of and methods for taking statistics. We cannot stress enough how providing accurate statistics makes the media's job easier, in turn providing additional recognition for your team. Season win-loss records and other notes about both teams are appreciated (e.g., how many points one team scored in a row, how many consecutive batters a pitcher retired, or how long the winning scoring drive was).

Some newspapers have developed forms to assist schools in reporting results. Filling out the form and faxing it to media outlets and following up with a phone call to ensure they received the fax, is becoming an appreciated form of reporting results to newspapers. Sample result reporting forms can be found at the end of this chapter (see pp. 59–63).

No Con Games

Never make up information about the game, especially names of players from the opposing school. Once, the sports editor of a newspaper in suburban Detroit took the information from the school calling in the results of a game and printed it. A call from an upset parent of the opponent the following day revealed that the person calling in the report made up the first names of players on that team. Consequently, that paper was very careful in future dealings with that school. Who were the losers? The kids.

Remember, like late and irregular callers, the media also keep track of purveyors of bad information, and that could affect future coverage of your teams.

BEING AVAILABLE

When you meet with the media before the season, let them know the best time for contacting you and your coaches. As the sport director, provide your home telephone number so the media can reach you in a pinch. Accessibility at home is a necessary evil of being a publicist, and most responsible media members do not abuse the privilege.

Always return phone calls to the media, and compel your coaches to meet with reporters following games. The media will understand if a coach wants to spend a few moments with the team, but while the majority of a coach's job for the day ends with the completion of the event, that end just marks the beginning for the media. Again, time is coverage, so don't keep them waiting.

GENERATING FEATURE IDEAS

If you ever have an idea for a feature story, don't hesitate to suggest it to a media outlet. Some newspapers set up times when they want athletic administrators and coaches to call with feature ideas, notes, records, unusual occurrences, and individual recognition information. Most outlets prefer this approach to getting the information via stringers as event results are called in. The type of media market you're in will dictate what, how, and when ideas will get used. In general, between 30 and 50 percent of these ideas become feature articles.

If you desire something bigger in a feature, either presenting unique information or taking a global approach can make a difference. Asking for a feature on your team's leading performer usually isn't enough. If you would like a feature on a team that normally receives less coverage than sports like football or basketball, suggesting a feature about the sport in the entire community, mentioning all schools involved, improves your chance of being published over asking for a feature about your school or team. And because you generated the idea, your school might be more prominently featured in the story.

Some ideas for stories include

- a team that is successful with no seniors or all freshmen,
- some players involved in an unusual play during a recent game,
- record-setting players,
- a group of players with exceptional grade point averages, or
- a player who has experienced an unusual life occurrence and how it has improved the individual's play and life.

Above all, avoid demanding coverage or features. You will only begin to alienate the media, hurting your kids in the process. Let the media determine the newsworthiness of your story, and if an advance feature is done on an event, follow up with a call to report the results. Nothing is more embarrassing to your school or a media outlet than to play up an upcoming event, and then fail to report the results.

TELLING PARENTS YOU ARE THE MEDIA CONTACT

If any aspect of promotion is a colossal waste of time, it is parents who call the media to complain about their team's coverage or lack thereof. Parents have little ability to positively affect their team's media coverage.

Some parents feel that ganging up on a media outlet by bombarding it with calls demanding coverage is effective. Unless something has been factually wrong with the coverage, this too is ineffective. Any stories that result from these calling chains are usually done simply to stop the phone calls and generate more hard feelings between the media outlet and school than the effort was worth.

During your preseason meetings inform the media that you will try to channel any concerns about their coverage through you, then talk with parents and coaches about your plan. If you set the table properly, you can have non-adversarial conversation with the media about this sensitive issue.

What Doesn't Work

A television sportscaster on a local radio talk shown once bemoaned the excessive calling campaign the parents of a school were conducting on behalf of a team. Of course, these comments generated phone calls to other talk shows in the town that started, "Why doesn't the TV station like our team?"

Newspapers also rightfully complain about parents calling in their kid's statistics. One parent was becoming famous for calling in only her daughter's statistics after games, raising questions about their legitimacy. That same student transferred to another school in the same community the next year and said during an interview that one of the reasons she transferred was that she thought she would get more media coverage. The reporter noted that the clip never made it on the air.

SUCCEEDING IN THE MEDIA INTERVIEW

A good media interview in the newspaper, on the radio, or on television can be a powerful communication tool for your school. A poor interview can cause innumerable problems. Regardless, all sport directors and coaches must face interviews, and taking the cue from some college or professional coaches and players who make a game of jerking the media around will only hurt you and your school in the long run.

Postgame Interviews for Your Coaches

This information is best communicated as a list of Do's and Don'ts:

Do's (in this order):

1. Be prompt in meeting with the media.
2. Be gracious.
3. Be honest.
4. Make comments in the best interest of educational athletics.
5. Be positive.
6. Acknowledge the play of the opponent positively.
7. Be a good sport.

Don'ts:

1. Keep the media waiting.
2. Belittle your team or the opponent.
3. Make negative comments toward game officials.
4. Say "no comment."

Being gracious doesn't mean you have to answer every question. If you, a coach, or a player encounter this situation, politely state that you don't wish to answer that question. You have that right, just as the reporter has the right to ask it. As mentioned previously, never say "no comment." It makes you look suspicious, and it's rude.

Always a Right Answer, Even Later

If you encounter a question that you can't answer at that time (which is different from one you could answer but don't), simply say so. If the questioner seeks information you can obtain, state that you will obtain an answer for them as soon as possible. Be sure, however, that you or your coaches hold up your end of the bargain.

What Gets Printed

Avoid feeling let down if all the information you or your coaches convey in the interview fails to get reported. After all, reporters translate what they perceive to be important into print, just as you make decisions about your program and coaches make decisions during games. Besides, one never knows whether the reporter put the information into the story initially, only to have it cut by an editor because of space restrictions. You also cannot know whether that reporter has a set agenda, and comments may only be used if they support that individual's mind-set.

No Negatives

Just as you should avoid using "no comment," avoid negative words like "can't," "didn't," "don't," and "won't." Keep the negative comments to yourself, and never say anything that will come back to haunt you.

Always on the Record

Unless you and the reporter agree in advance that certain comments will be kept in confidence, plan that everything said is "on the record." Still, most reporters covering high school athletics are not headhunters. Work under that assumption until they prove otherwise. Most of these people love high school athletics as much as you do, and they treat it differently than college or professional sports. Some media members, however, feel they must act *big time*, and the only way they know how to do that is by being critical.

Policies for Interviews

You can set local policies for postgame and other interviews, starting with the comfort level for each individual coach. Some have no problem performing interviews on the playing surface within moments of a contest's conclusion. Others prefer to have a few moments with the team in the dressing room before facing the media.

During your preseason meeting with the media, inform them of the postgame and other interview preferences for your school or individual coaches. Encourage coaches to be consistent, so the media will know what to expect when attending your events.

Some state tournament events issue guidelines, set by the tournament sponsor, that they expect coaches and media to follow for pre- and postgame interviews. Because of the sheer number of media at a tournament center, practicing your regular-season routine may be nearly impossible.

Some of those policies may prevent coaches and players from being interviewed on the playing surface after a game; delegate that a specific room be used for all interviews, with the losing coach always doing the first interview. Or require the winning coach of a game to visit with live statewide radio and television networks before doing any other interviews. Tournament sites often conduct formal press conferences, asking a coach to bring certain players who had some kind of impact on the game and are the most newsworthy in the media's eyes.

Although coaches still have the right to bring who they want (or not bring players at all), it is good public relations to comply with the request rather than grabbing only team captains or seniors. But if youngsters have trouble in that setting, coaches should not force them into an interview.

A current NBA player literally took classes on public speaking and was consistently coached on interviewing while in college to help overcome a speech impediment that could have caused him to be labeled a poor interview.

HANDLING THE CRISIS SITUATION

When a crisis occurs, such as a catastrophic injury, death of an athlete, or the suspension of some players or coaches, the time you and your coaches have taken to cultivate the local media should build a rapport that will pay off. What can happen in a crisis, however, is that you may encounter a reporter you haven't dealt with before; the sports reporter may be pulled off the coverage and replaced by a newswriter.

Experience tells us that many sports writers could cover a news story (just ask Al Michaels of ABC or Bob Ley of ESPN about covering the earthquake at the World Series in San Francisco), but the reverse is not always true. A newswriter assigned to cover a crisis involving your athletic program may have little knowledge of sports, is only interested in the *news* angle in the story, and lacks that day-to-day relationship that you have established with the writer assigned to your team or school.

Apply Same Rules

Proceed cautiously, but remember that the basic principles of the general interview still apply. Honesty is still the best policy, but if you don't have the right answer to a question, promise to get it as soon as possible. Never jeopardize your credibility by making up an answer.

Develop a Game Plan

Before doing interviews in a crisis situation, determine the message you and your coaches want to convey; the timetable for delivering that message (i.e., if *A* occurs, then we proceed to *B*); the individual(s) you want delivering the message; and who internally should have the message. Also consider vehicles for delivering the message and constantly evaluate the situation, tailoring your comments accordingly.

Do not panic in a crisis. Avoid making comments that might appear in a headline or unnecessarily create hurt feelings. The media looks for an emotionally charged comment, and that kind of comment can only harm you. Taking the high road, no matter how you feel when the notebook opens or the microphone is thrust in your face, is always the best course of action.

HANDLING MEDIA AT HOME GAMES

The final piece in the publicity puzzle is how your school services the media at its home events.

Media Seating Arrangements

First and foremost, always provide seating arrangements for the media. The press area should be clean and provide counter space and access to electrical and telephone outlets.

The area should not be a haven for non-workers; rather, it should promote a professional working environment (i.e., keep school board members and parents out). This is most easily accomplished at football stadiums and in gymnasiums, where more space can be set aside. Also ensure that this area allows reporters to arrive on their timetable. Don't force a media person to show up an hour or two early and threaten that individual with not getting a seat if they fail to comply—they might not show up!

But It's a *Press* Box!

A reporter called one day to tell his tale of covering a football playoff game. After calling the athletic director of the host school early in the week, he was told he'd have no problem getting in and having a seat in the press box. Upon arrival, the reporter worked his way to the top of the stands to the press box entrance, where he identified himself to the security guard, who told him the box was for school administrators and selected members of the team's dad's club to sit in.

"But it's a *press* box," the reporter replied.

The guard referred the reporter to the athletic director, who was standing on the field. The athletic director told the reporter that he should have called to make arrangements. After jogging the athletic director's memory of their conversation earlier in the week, he received a pass to the press box. Upon entry, he found the media standing in the back while the administrators and dad's club members filled the seats at the counter.

A lesson in poor media relations: Make your press box just that, not a sky box for your administration and others.

Equal Treatment

Attempt to treat all media equally. Sometimes placement of electrical and telephone outlets required by radio stations during the game imposes on your ability to succeed. Still, avoid treating hometown media differently than visiting media. Provide adequate working space and creature comforts for both. Remember, you have to make an impression on both parties, and consistency is probably the highest aim you can hope to achieve.

Telephones

Your press area should enable you to install several telephone outlets in case a radio station wishes to broadcast a game from your facility. The stations are responsible for their own installations. Also consider having your own telephone installed in the press box, especially at fields in remote locations. This phone could be an extension of an existing telephone number at the school, and though you may have a similar charge for installing the line, the monthly costs should be lower than a new number. Contact your local telephone company for details.

Delegate a responsible person to ensure a telephone is plugged in and working during the event, and that the phone instrument is unplugged and removed from the press box at the event's conclusion. Give the media access to this phone after games to file reports. You can also use it to report results to media not in attendance and for emergencies. This phone should not be accessible to the public.

At indoor events, it is not as essential to install a special phone in the press area. Instead, be ready to direct a media member to an area in your building away from the crowd (not a pay phone if at all possible!), like your office, a coach's office, or a secretary's desk.

Again, remember that when the game is over and your job is winding down, a reporter's job may be just beginning. It is an inconvenience sometimes, but a professional courtesy to allow writers the time they need to write and file their stories. Telling writers they will have to finish their stories somewhere else and find a telephone outside the building will not score any public relations points. It's worth it to allow someone to hang around for those few extra moments, regardless of postgame plans.

Hospitality

Media appreciate simple hospitality when it can be shown. It need be nothing more than complimentary hot and cold beverages and finger foods in the press box or other designated area. Some schools go all out, providing salads, sandwiches, and other snacks. You decide much your school does, but even simple efforts create fond memories.

Admission Policies

You may wish to develop a policy for media admission to events, publicizing it through your preseason meetings with them. Often, the media will bring only working people, but once in a while, a spouse or others may ride the coattails of a working person into the event. A true professional reporter will not try to take advantage of your hospitality and will pay for additional people they bring. You do not need to accommodate this person in your press area unless you have ample space, certainly not at the expense of another working person.

You can add another nice touch by setting aside a special parking area for the press (if a portion of the parking lot can be secured for this purpose). Just inform the media of its availability in advance. Some schools even develop pocket press cards, a sample of which appears in Figure 4.7, which they send at the beginning of the school year to all area media that may cover their teams. Some media already have identification from their outlet, and some states use local or state police press identification passes.

Media Host or Specialist

Your team statistician could be your media specialist, handling some of the simple, yet time-consuming work (like making postgame calls and preparing rosters, stats, and schedules) that could pay off in recognition for your school and its athletes and could also be a valuable experience for the individual you appoint. Many professional and college team publicists started as statistician/publicist for their high school teams.

Whether the specialist is a student or staff person, select a responsible individual who can build a strong rapport with the media. That person could be charged with the following duties:

- Making postgame calls to the media
- Providing the media with schedules, rosters, statistics, game notes, and other information during the season
- Serving as press box host for home games and providing the media with programs, lineups, and refreshments
- Escorting the media to the designated postgame interview area

PRESS 199_-9_
Jefferson High School
Jets

Full courtesies of press facilities at all home athletic events are extended to

Robert Jones, Madison Press

No. 001 Charles Baer
Athletic Director

(Actual Size—3 1/4 x 2 1/4)

Figure 4.7 Sample pocket press card.

WORKING WITH RADIO AND TELEVISION ORIGINATIONS AT YOUR GAMES

Times were that seemingly every radio station carried high school sporting events, and television was out of the question for anything but *major* athletic contests. But times have changed. In some areas it's a luxury to have a game on radio, and cable television brings several prep events into living rooms every week. You need a working understanding of each of these areas because you'll probably encounter both eventually.

Radio

On a Friday night drive in some parts of the country, you can still scan the radio dial and pick up dozens of high school athletic event broadcasts, especially in states comprised of many small- to medium-sized radio markets. But in larger cities with multiple high schools, hearing even the scores of high school games is rare. The face of radio has changed dramatically in the past two decades, but the development of talk radio—sports talk specifically—is beginning to open the door again for stations originating high school athletic events.

The format change to talk radio makes sports fit again, but even though high school broadcasts have returned in some markets, emphasis still tends toward higher-profile sports, such as basketball (boys and girls) and football. Small town stations, however, still broadcast everything they can get a microphone to, especially if the local team is in a state tournament.

Telephone Costs

Aside from format considerations, telephone deregulation was probably one of the worst things that could happen to the broadcasting of high school athletic events in the 1980s. Deregulation drove the costs of installing the necessary telephone service in many communities to nearly $150 to do one game at one site. Stations became more and more restricted, especially about covering away contests.

New Transmission Options

But alternative technologies appear to be filling the gap. Improvements in cellular telephone coverage give stations the opportunity to make a one-time investment in cellular equipment, and charges for cellular phone air time have averaged out to be lower than if they had to install a phone line everywhere they went.

Other equipment enables a radio station to set up in your press box and send its signal to a scanner hooked up to an existing telephone (your telephone nearby in your facility), which then sends the broadcast back to the station. If a station wishes to come to your school to originate a game using this method, it generally lets you know that when making arrangements to come to your building. Just make sure the station doesn't leave you with long-distance charges!

Local games in some communities still use a *marti* unit, a transmitter set up at the game site to send the origination back to the station where it is rebroadcast over the air.

Co-Op Opportunities

If your school is a member of a conference where many or all the schools have radio stations broadcasting their games, you might consider bringing those stations together to set up what are referred to as *co-op* lines. In a co-op, the radio station following each school installs telephone lines for its broadcast, as well as for those of visiting teams. This way, a station only installs two lines for that sport (at least for conference play) for the entire season, knowing that when it travels to an away game, a line awaits them. This approach is also easier for you because a co-op line is installed at the beginning of the season, rather than having the telephone company come back several times during the year to install a new telephone line for a single game.

Self-Provided Phone Service

If stations aren't interested in a co-op, you might consider getting into the telephone business yourself. To accommodate visiting radio stations, you might install a line yourself in your press box or gymnasium, then charge stations a per-game fee for its use. You would determine the rate by figuring out how many visiting stations would use the phone during a season, then dividing it into your cost of installing and maintaining the line.

For example, if you have five home football games that you are sure will attract visiting radio stations, divide the installation cost and monthly service charges for the period you will have the line (about three months) by five. This charge might work out to be about $45 or $50 a game if your installation cost was $150, the monthly service charge to maintain the line was $20, and five stations used the line. Just make sure the stations bill long distance charges back to their company.

This approach can be a public relations coup if you're sure you can do it without losing money (in fact, you could make a few dollars along the way). Some colleges and state high school athletic associations work out similar arrangements for their major events. It saves money for the stations and reduces headaches for the sponsoring agency. The only potential for trouble comes in chasing down stations for payment and long-distance charges. You can minimize even this risk by withholding access to your courtesy line until stations have paid you in advance and have been told to reverse long-distance charges.

Work Space

When a radio station comes to your school to originate a game, provide them table space in an area where they can view the game without obstruction, and ensure electrical service at that location. If the event is outdoors, stations appreciate your provision of shelter from the elements, such as press box seats.

Limits on Broadcast Crew Size

Don't hesitate to limit the number of people radio stations bring with them. In general, stations travel with two people, sometimes three. You have the right to limit how many people they pass through the gate.

Family Affair

Another favorite story concerns the broadcaster who engineered, kept score, and did all the announcing of the game himself at a state tournament event, but kept his wife and kid with him at courtside. Some media think their drivers, families, or anyone else should get in free with the *favor* they are doing by broadcasting your game. Some people try anything to abuse the privilege. Just be sure to treat visiting radio stations the same way you treat your home radio station.

Information to Provide

Provide visiting radio stations with the same information you would your home station: scores, rosters, statistics, and pronunciations.

You may have been surprised to see *pronunciations* in the previous paragraph, but our diverse world presents name pronunciation challenges. Radio and public address announcers from other schools will appreciate typed phonetic lists of your players' names.

Television

Television is more intensive to accommodate than radio, but it can also be a great source of exposure. Crews need to set up multiple cameras, and announcers require extra table space for replay monitors and the production assistants who sit next to them.

Equipment Locations

Most TV originations take three to four cameras. Two cameras are generally located up high, in or atop a press box or the highest row of bleachers; the other cameras are hand-held and may be located on the field or in an end zone in an elevated position. Announcers work from a booth in the press box or at a table on the floor. You also need to designate a location where the remote unit (truck) will park and prepare for the possibility that the unit will want to hook into your site's electrical system.

The most common originations of high school events on television use local cable systems, which has evolved into a slick package with multiple cameras, replays, and graphics as technology has become more affordable. Occasionally, local on-air stations originate games as well.

Unless you have a television production class at your school, this medium is not something you'll get into yourself. If you do, many of the same principles from radio apply here.

TV's Effect on the Game

Unless the game is a rare live broadcast, you won't have to worry about the origination affecting the game. If the broadcast is live, you may be asked to adjust the starting time anywhere from 3 to 7 minutes, and to position a person at the scorer's table to alert officials about television breaks. In general though, you won't see television timeouts.

Rights Fees

Some schools and leagues have begun charging *rights fees* for their games, which are common for state tournaments, but discourage stations from broadcasting local games. Rights fees are monetary charges a station pays to the school or game organizer for the opportunity to broadcast that game. Considering the small amount of money your school could generate from these fees (unless you occupy a highly competitive position and several stations want to broadcast your games badly enough to be willing to pay big money for the opportunity), stay away from rights fees. If you do impose these fees, remember that you only control broadcast rights at your home games! The station you grant exclusive rights to at home may face competition on the road from other stations in your community.

OBTAINING FREE PUBLICITY

Publicity includes efforts at promoting your sport program that are within your control. They represent readily available opportunities crying out for you to use them to communicate your messages. The type of community you live in and your school facilities and philosophies will dictate your publicity possibilities and limitations. Although these opportunities are free from monetary expense, they often require an investment of time and energy.

Marquee Ads

A great opportunity for free publicity awaits you on the commercial strips in your town. Many businesses sport message centers, or marquees, in front of their businesses to attract customers. You can probably get occasional free use of those message boards to publicize your program and your athletes' achievements.

The message can be fairly simple, as you can see from the example in Figure 4.8. You can promote upcoming events, recognize a student for a great performance, and simply send a good luck message to a team. When you have a team advancing in a tournament, many businesses hop on the band-wagon with good luck messages on their marquees. The gas station that owns the marquee shown in Figure 4.9 congratulating a player of the week, also buys ad time on a local radio station to convey the same message.

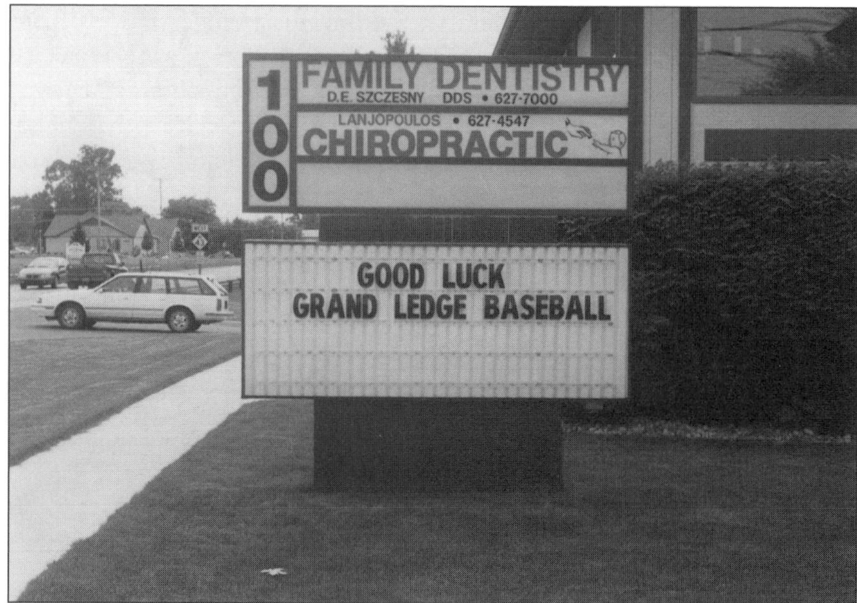

Figure 4.8 "Good Luck Team" marquee.

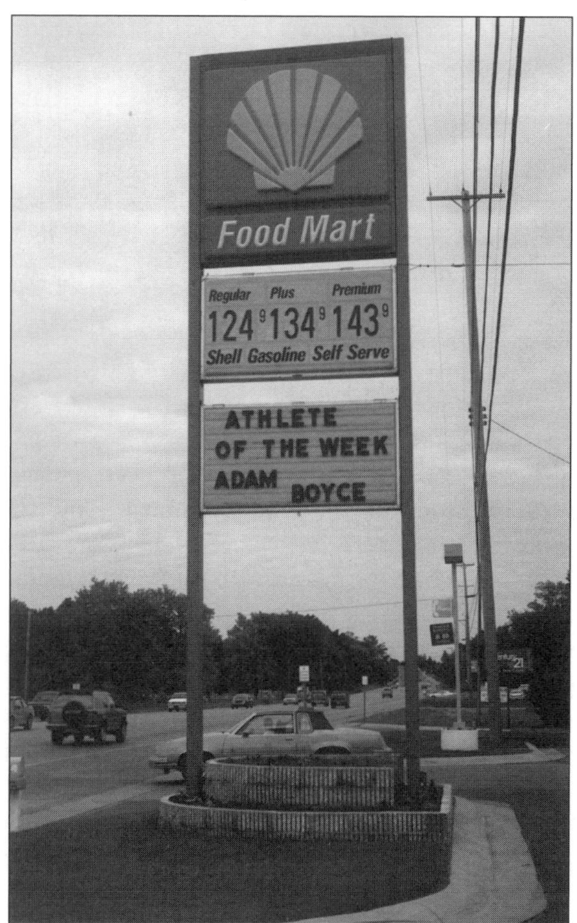

Figure 4.9 Marquee sample.

Before the athletic season begins, you may wish to contact selected businesses to discuss the possibility of using their message centers to help promote school teams. These messages must be limited to only a handful of words. Remember, people who see marquee messages pass by those signs in their cars at anywhere from 25 to 55 miles per hour!

By using marquee messages, you involve area businesses in an activity that promotes community pride. All they have to do is change the message occasionally; they don't have a cash outlay. People in the community tend to patronize businesses that are involved with school programs. The business receives the benefit of being associated with the school program, hoping to turn some of that association into sales.

On-Campus Opportunities

Moving to opportunities in your building, the school marquee (if you have one) is right at your fingertips, and many schools regularly use it to promote athletic events. The daily public address announcement period represents another possibility to promote athletic events, and don't overlook the public address announcements at your athletic events (see sample in Figure 4.10) for promoting other activities and achievements.

Next Week's Events in Panther Sports

(Read 1x per half at football game vs. Westfield)

Here's a look at the Panther home sports schedule for next week. On Tuesday, the girls volleyball teams host Westfield with the junior varsity game beginning at 6 p.m., and the boys soccer team has a match against Plainfield at 4 p.m. that same day. On Thursday, the cross country teams compete in the Panther Invitational at Frosty Top Golf Course at 4 p.m., and the girls volleyball teams take on Gas City with the junior varsity game at 6 p.m. The homecoming football game with Greenwood is scheduled for Saturday night at 7:30 p.m., here at Murphy Stadium. Support your Panthers next week!

Figure 4.10 Sample public address announcement.

Some schools use *ribbon boards*, electronic message centers around the building, or television monitors in strategic locations to provide messages to students. These represent additional promotional venues. If these message centers are available during athletic events, they're as good as the public address system for spreading the word about your program.

INVOLVING YOUR PERSONNEL

We have explored potential roles for your coaches, athletes, and others within the organization throughout this chapter. To summarize, your people can serve

- in speaking roles, either through internal or external speakers bureaus or through presentations, such as preseason meetings and homeroom programs;
- in media relations, either as a representative designated to call in results, as a host to the media for home events when a number of media attend, as one who types and distributes rosters, schedules, and statistics to the media, in interview roles; and
- in publicity, as a contact to local businesses to solicit use of their message centers, or as a script writer for announcements used for homeroom and in-game purposes.

EVALUATING YOUR PUBLIC RELATIONS EFFORTS

Of all the pieces of the promotion puzzle, public relations is the hardest in which to measure the actual results. You won't be able to see a direct effect on attendance. You will, however, perceive a general sense of the sport program's reputation within your school and throughout the community.

Using the evaluation forms presented in chapter 3, you can create a category to record all feedback you received for a given endeavor. Keep track of the phone calls you made or received regarding a particular topic, and keep any letters you may receive. Seek input from others in attendance formally (possibly a survey) or informally (telephone or personal conversation). Any documentation you can produce is critical.

If you neglect this evaluation, feedback may not come until you attempt the same public relations project a year later, and the people you contact finally give you an opinion—pro or con. Unfortunately, many people choose this method to let you know what they think of what you've done.

Summary

To build positive public relations,

1. remember that any good public relations program begins with positive internal public relations,
2. create a positive feeling among your staff and internal constituents to give you a group of ambassadors to support your community efforts,
3. use media relations' basic Who-What-When formula,
4. access opportunities for free publicity through non-media avenues,
5. include a variety of individuals in executing your public relations program, and
6. remember that measuring your public relations efforts is more difficult than measuring the effectiveness of any other part of your promotion program; whatever documentation you can obtain is essential.

Form 4.1 Instructions for Reporting Results for Cross-Country, Gymnastics, Skiing, Swimming, and Track and Field Events

In any sport where time or a score is used to rank individuals, give the name of the event with the names of the top finishers listed in the order of finish followed by the time, distance, or points totaled. Time should be the official time (i.e., if fully automatic times (FAT) are used, give the time to the hundredth of a second). *Never state a hand time beyond a tenth of a second.*

For team scoring, simply list the final team scores in order.

Here is a sample summary. Because of the many different events in gymnastics, swimming, and track and field, we are not including a sample summary sheet.

100-meter dash

1. Michael Lewis (Mt. Pleasant)	:11.3
2. John Figg (Saginaw-Heritage)	:11.5
3. John Mitchell (Midland-Dow)	:11.6

Form 4.2 Sample Result Reporting Form for Baseball/Softball

Here is a sample linescore followed by an explanation.

Kalamazoo-Central	1	0	2	0	0	0	1	4	7	2
Jackson-Northwest	1	0	0	0	0	2	0	3	6	1

Brian Jones and Bill Merriweather; Joe Smith, Phil Richards (3) and Jim DeMarco; WP: Jones (4-1); LP: Smith (1-1); HRs: (Kalamazoo-Central) Don Fischer (2)

Explanation: The visiting team is always listed on top, the home team on the bottom. Give the score by innings, and then the totals of runs, hits, and errors. Underneath the score, give the pitching/catching combinations beginning with the visiting team. Always give the starting pitcher, then the relief pitchers as they appear, and note the inning in which they entered the game. The word “and” is always used to separate pitchers and catchers. Put substitute catchers into the same order as the pitchers. After the batteries, give the winning pitcher and his/her record, doing the same for the losing pitcher.

Variations: Some papers may want saves, and then hits beginning with singles, then doubles, and so on. Always have team records available.

A sample blank form appears on the next page.

Baseball/Softball Result Reporting Form

(Be sure to use first and last names for all players.)

Score by innings	1	2	3	4	5	6	7	R	H	E
Visitor: ________	___	___	___	___	___	___	___	___	___	___
Home: ________	___	___	___	___	___	___	___	___	___	___

Visitor pitchers (starter): ____________________

(reliever): ____________________ (inning) ________

(reliever): ____________________ (inning) ________

Visitor catchers (starter): ____________________

(reliever): ____________________ (inning) ________

Home pitchers (starter): ____________________

(reliever): ____________________ (inning) ________

(reliever): ____________________ (inning) ________

Home catchers (starter): ____________________

(reliever): ____________________ (inning) ________

Winning pitcher: ____________________ Record: __________

Losing pitcher: ____________________ Record: __________

Home runs (give team, player, number of HRs for season): ____________________

____

Season records: visitor __________ home __________

Conference records (if conference game): visitor __________ home __________

Notes: ____

____

____

____

____

____

____

____

____

Form 4.3 Sample Result Reporting Form for Basketball

Here is a sample box score. The visiting team is always listed first.

Battle Creek-St. Philip	15	30	20	20	85
Galesburg-Augusta	15	5	10	10	40

Battle Creek-St. Philip: Paul Morgan 2-4 5-6 9, John Beatty 10-13 8-8 31, Steve Babik 5-7 9-9 22, Carl Ullrich 5-9 0-1 10, Jack Moss 6-9 1-1 13. Totals 28-42 23-25 85

Galesburg-Augusta: Steve Hettinger 4-9 5-6 13, Joe Carson 5-10 1-1 11, John Johnson 1-5 1-4 4, Bill Winninger 3-4 2-2 8, Michael Cooper 2-2 0-0 4. Totals 15-30 9-13 40

Three-point goals: Beatty 3-4, Babik 3-5, Carson 1-2

Explanation: Give the amount of points scored in each quarter for each team first. Generally, you will be asked for one team at a time. Then give the box score for the visiting team. As a rule, use full names though some will ask for last names only with initials when a team has two players with the same last name. Give the field goals attempted and made, the free throws attempted and made, and then the point total. Since the three-point goal is in use, we have added a line for three-point goals made in our sample.

Variations: Some papers will ask for just the field goals and free throws made instead of attempts and shots made. Other papers may ask for more statistics like rebounds, assists, and the individual leaders in those categories, while others may ask for all stats in all categories for all individuals. *Be ready to give them everything they could want.*

A sample blank form appears on the following pages.

Basketball Result Reporting Form

(Be sure to use first and last names for all players.)

Score by quarters	1	2	3	4	OT	OT	Total
Visitor:______________	___	___	___	___	___	___	_____
Home: ______________	___	___	___	___	___	___	_____

Visitor scoring:

Full name	Field goals att	Field goals made	Free throws att	Free throws made	Total points
____________________	____	____	____	____	______
____________________	____	____	____	____	______
____________________	____	____	____	____	______
____________________	____	____	____	____	______
____________________	____	____	____	____	______
____________________	____	____	____	____	______
____________________	____	____	____	____	______
____________________	____	____	____	____	______
____________________	____	____	____	____	______
____________________	____	____	____	____	______
____________________	____	____	____	____	______
____________________	____	____	____	____	______
____________________	____	____	____	____	______
____________________	____	____	____	____	______
Totals	____	____	____	____	______

Home scoring:

Full name	Field goals att	Field goals made	Free throws att	Free throws made	Total points
____________________	____	____	____	____	______
____________________	____	____	____	____	______
____________________	____	____	____	____	______
____________________	____	____	____	____	______
____________________	____	____	____	____	______
____________________	____	____	____	____	______
____________________	____	____	____	____	______
____________________	____	____	____	____	______
____________________	____	____	____	____	______
____________________	____	____	____	____	______
____________________	____	____	____	____	______
____________________	____	____	____	____	______
____________________	____	____	____	____	______
____________________	____	____	____	____	______
Totals	____	____	____	____	______

Three-point goals: ______________________________

Visitor rebounds: ______ Individual leaders: ______________________________

____

Home rebounds: ______ Individual leaders: ______________________________

____

Visitor assists: ______ Individual leaders: ______________________________

Home assists: ______ Individual leaders: ______________________________

Turnovers: visitor ______ home ______

Total fouls: visitor ______ home ______ fouled out (name, school): _________

____

Technical fouls (name, school): ______________________________

Season records: visitor __________ home __________

Conference records (if conference game): visitor __________ home __________

Notes: ______________________________

____

____

____

____

____

____

____

Junior varsity score: visitor _____ home ______

Chapter 5
Promotion Through Printed Materials

In this chapter, you will learn

1. how to gain newspaper exposure, beyond specific event reports;
2. how to develop an aggressive print campaign that incorporates schedule cards, posters, game programs, and alternative print forms;
3. how to determine editorial/advertising balances;
4. how to determine advertising ratios and the variety of options you have for printing materials; and
5. how to evaluate your print promotion plan.

Your most important promotional duties are publicizing event schedules and recognizing your participants. Getting this information to the media in a timely manner is important, but nothing tops constant public exposure. The media's ability to provide this exposure is limited: Most newspapers print entire season schedules only in football and basketball—and then only once a year. Many newspapers relegate other sports' schedules to the prep daily or weekly sports calendars on scoreboard pages.

HOW PRINT LITERATE ARE YOU?

Some sport directors, pressed for time and resources, set a low standard for the community with poorly produced print materials about the athletic program.

Frequently, however, the sheet of handwritten paper that serves as a poster promoting an upcoming season or piece of folded paper containing rosters so small that readers need a magnifying glass results from a lack of knowledge about printing and how an effective print promotion program can be put together.

Use Figure 5.1 to determine how print literate you are and to explore how to integrate print promotions into your program.

How Print Literate Are You?

Here are a few questions to test your knowledge of printed materials:

1. A pocket schedule is generally sized to fit in
   a. your back pocket
   b. your wallet
   c. a pocket pita
   d. none of the above
2. Fifty-pound text describes what?
   a. the weight of this book
   b. the strength of fishing line
   c. the thickness of the paper you are printing on
3. When paying for a printed piece, your advertising costs should be
   a. broken into equal segments so all advertisers cover only the printing costs
   b. divided so that the advertising covers only half the printing costs—you'll make up the difference when you sell them at the game
   c. divided so that the piece is paid for once you reach a designed point (one-half to three-quarters) in available sales. The additional income becomes a source of revenue for your school.
4. What is an economical approach to printing schedule posters or pocket schedules?
   a. Print a separate piece for each sport, listing the varsity and sub-varsity schedules.
   b. Print one piece with all schedules.
   c. Print a separate piece for each level of each sport.
5. What common numbers are game programs generally set up in?
   a. one sheet of paper
   b. two pages at a time
   c. four- or eight-page sections
   d. none of the above
6. What is a signature?
   a. your John Hancock on something
   b. your employer's name on your paycheck
   c. how a section of printed material is set up
7. What is the major difference between an in-house and a commercial printer?
   a. The in-house printer generally involves in-school personnel from start to finish.
   b. The commercial printer prints commercials.
   c. The in-house printer prints houses.
8. Desktop publishing is
   a. a copier sitting on your desk
   b. using computer software to handle the typesetting and graphics of your printed materials without jobbing it out to a printer
   c. a new way to build desks

(continued)

Figure 5.1 How print literate are you?

9. How do you determine the cost of a printing project?
   a. Show a sample to different printers and solicit bids.
   b. Pick a number out of the air.
   c. Ask just one printer for a cost.
10. What is the advantage to bidding out your printing?
    a. It's a great way to meet new people.
    b. You are assured a market-driven cost.
    c. No one bids out jobs any more.
11. What is the best way to provide copy to your printer for typesetting?
    a. a hand-written sheet with information
    b. a typewritten sheet
    c. a computer file on disk generated by a word processing program
    d. none of the above
12. What is the ideal ad-to-copy mix in a souvenir program?
    a. 75% ads; 25% rosters, schedules, and pictures
    b. no ads—100% rosters, schedules, and pictures
    c. an even mix (50/50)
    d. whatever you feel like
13. True or false: A full-page ad generates more revenue than a page full of smaller ads.
14. What is a proof?
    a. The proof is in the pudding.
    b. a draft of your typeset copy for you to make corrections on
    c. documentation that you did something

Answers: 1. *b* 2. *c* 3. *c* 4. *b* 5. *c* 6. *c* 7. *a* 8. *b* 9. *a* 10. *b* 11. *c* 12. *c* 13. *False* 14. *b*

Figure 5.1 *(continued)*

NEWSPAPER PROMOTIONS

Newspapers devote only so much space to sports, and as we saw in media relations, getting everything into the paper without having to pay for it is nearly impossible.

We do not advocate the radical approach some professional and college teams have taken, actually purchasing space for their own publicists to write game reports. Cost is prohibitive, and these efforts may strain relations, reducing the likelihood that your program obtains the space it deserves.

However, a spin-off of that idea can inform people of your upcoming events. Colleges and professional teams frequently include newspaper ads in the cost of a corporation's event sponsorship. Chapter 8 explores in depth the different aspects of developing sponsorship, but the print portion ties in well here.

Such an ad need not be large. In fact, if a local business wishes to be identified with a team or group of teams, you might encourage it to take out a small *clip and save* newspaper ad, including schedules of teams that might not otherwise get them published.

This approach may compete with schedule cards and posters, described later in this chapter, but at a time when businesses want to find a unique promotion niche, you might find that some would prefer to help you promote your program through the paper rather than through schedule cards and posters. In fact, many businesses involve themselves only in specific types of advertising, and a newspaper ad might be the only way some could help promote your program. A sample of such an ad is shown in Figure 5.2.

This is a sample of an ad set up for a newspaper with six columns across. It is 4 inches deep. It could cost an advertiser anywhere from $20 to $100 in a weekly newspaper, or from $30 to $150 in a daily newspaper.

Clip & Save

BOLTON BULLDOGS
199_ FOOTBALL
SCHEDULE

Sept. 2 - at Central
Sept. 9 - Hamilton
Sept. 16 - Lake City
Sept. 23 - Grand Junction
Sept. 30 - at Wishywak
Oct. 7 - Belding (Homecoming)
Oct. 14 - at Jonesville
Oct. 21 - at Smithville
Oct. 28 - Eastern (Parents' Night)

All home games start at 8 p.m.

Compliments of

Dairy Whip

2525 E. Beltline

(Next to Bulldog Field)

Figure 5.2 Sample ad.

PRINTED SCHEDULES

After newspaper promotions, the most common method of getting the word out about team schedules is a card or poster. Pocket schedules and posters serve as constant reminders of the school program and when games are going to be played. It may be your most cost-effective promotion tool.

Pocket Schedules

Pocket schedules have long been popular for promoting a single sport or an entire sports season. Many schools view the athletic program as a whole and publish sports schedules the same way. An all-sports schedule, published three times a year, is a great way to promote all sports and all levels of those sports equally. However, the school philosophy and tradition of a particular sport may demand a single-sport pocket schedule, and we explore both types here.

All-Sports Card

A complete pocket schedule lists the varsity and subvarsity schedules, including all starting times and at least the name of the head coach. A sample panel of a single sport's presentation on an all-sports schedule appears in Figure 5.3.

The all-sports pocket schedule is an accordion-fold style that should fit into a wallet. In general, you should depict an advertiser on the final panel of the schedule. When the schedule is folded correctly, the advertiser has a 50/50 chance of its message being seen by someone holding it.

Advertisers. You can also print the accordion-fold pocket schedule so that several advertisers can participate. When laying out the copy, duplicate all the schedules and front-panel artwork, then include a different advertiser on each back panel. Or include a variety of ads throughout the schedule. Remember that interior ads cannot be very large—probably no more than one-quarter of a panel—and are not as valuable to the advertiser. Most advertisers value being the only one appearing on a given printed unit.

Size. We base this discussion on printing an 11- by 17-inch sheet of paper, but you may set up on something bigger or smaller depending on your printer's capabilities. Printing on both sides of paper this size allows you to create five schedules each, having a finished folded size of about 2 1/5 by 3 3/8 inches.

This setup produces a 10-panel schedule (five panels on each side of the sheet). Using the front panel for a cover design and the back for an ad (see Figure 5.4) leaves you eight panels on which to print schedules.

Paper Weight. Because these schedules are to be folded and carried in pockets, purses, and wallets, as well as displayed in stacks, you should use fairly light paper stock, probably not exceeding the standard weight used in photocopiers. A professional printer would probably recommend 50-pound paper.

Varsity Football

Sept. 1	at Millersburg (7:00 p.m.)
Sept. 8	WACHOVIA* (7:30 p.m.)
Sept. 15	GAS CITY* (7:30 p.m.)
Sept. 22	at Bloomington* (8:00 p.m.)
Sept. 29	at Monroeville (8:00 p.m.)
Oct. 5	BUGGSVILLE* (Homecoming) (7:30 p.m.)
Oct. 12	Bakersfield Central (at Mountain Dome) (8:00 p.m.)
Oct. 19	MOUNT FORESTER* (7:30 p.m.)
Oct. 26	BELLEVILLE* (Parents' Night) (7:30 p.m.)

Home games in CAPITALS. All home games played at Murphy Field.
*Denotes Northwestern Conference games
Coach: Ben Sigler

Junior Varsity Football

Aug. 31	MILLERSBURG (7:00 p.m.)
Sept. 7	at Wachovia* (7:00 p.m.)
Sept. 14	at Gas City* (7:00 p.m.)
Sept. 21	BLOOMINGTON* (7:00 p.m.)
Sept. 28	MONROEVILLE (7:00 p.m.)
Oct. 4	at Buggsville* (6:00 p.m.)
Oct. 11	at Bakersfield Central (6:30 p.m.)
Oct. 19	MOUNT FORESTER* (5:00 p.m.)
Oct. 26	BELLEVILLE* (5:00 p.m.)

Home games in CAPITALS. All home games played at Murphy Field.
*Denotes Northwestern Conference games
Coach: William Johnson

Figure 5.3 Single-sport presentation.

Single-Sport Card

The single-sport card is more attractive than the all-sports card, but is more commonly used by professional and college teams than high schools. Generally, producing a single-sport card at a school is the direct result of a single-sport booster club or benefactor, usually for high-profile varsity teams. But the single-sport card can also be a political football. Anything done to highlight a single sport has the potential to make participants of other sports, and their parents, feel like second-class citizens.

Format. A single-sport card generally has an action photograph on one side, perhaps a top returning player or players, and the name of the school, sport, and year of the upcoming season. Names of featured players occasionally appear on the same side of the card, but such information is generally printed beneath the schedule on the flip side. Figure 5.5 illustrates how a number of cards can be produced from each sheet of paper, and how the ad on each card can be changed to represent different advertisers.

For a high school, printing single-sport cards in more than one color is a luxury. When adding a second color, schools often select the darker of their colors. Sometimes, schools use a two-color imprint on the picture side and a one-color imprint on the back.

Size. To fit easily in a pocket or wallet, these cards are usually about the size of a credit card. Using an 11- by 17-inch sheet, you could probably get 25

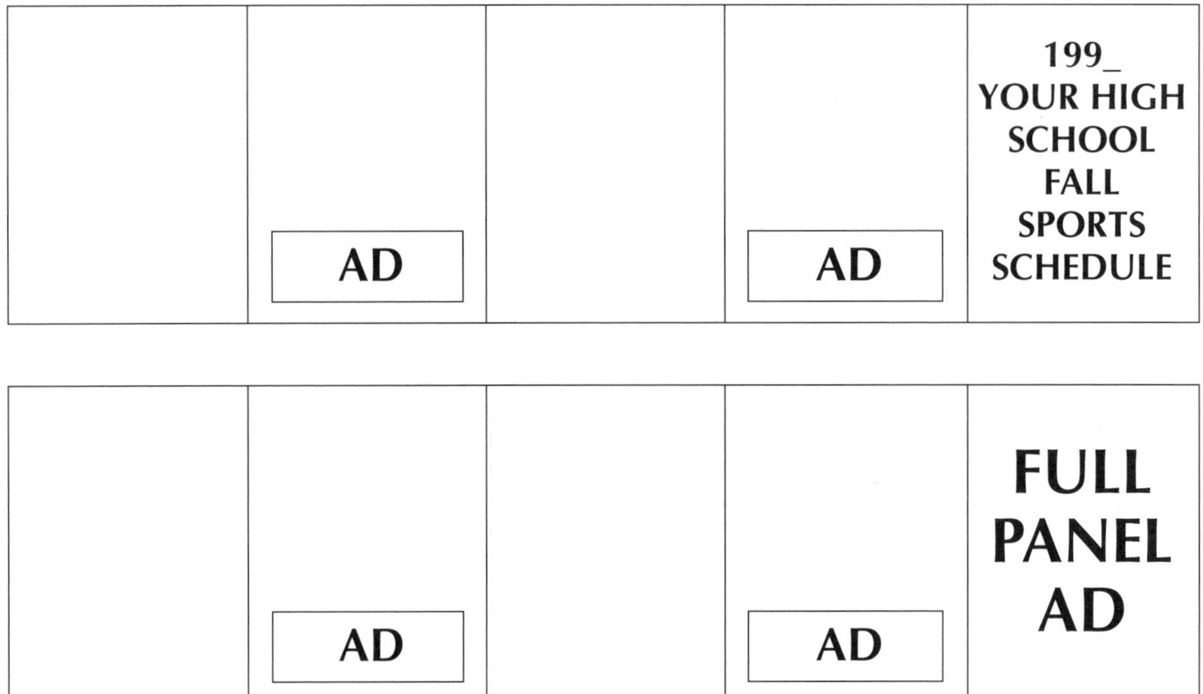

Figure 5.4 Layout of 10-panel card.

cards from a single sheet. Because so many individual cards come from a single sheet, you can include a variety of boosters, not only getting more businesses involved and identified with your program, but also lowering the cost to potential advertisers.

Stock. The single-sport card is printed on a heavier stock of paper, generally what printers call a *cover* stock, in the 80- to 100-pound range. The stock may have a flat finish on both sides or have a glossy finish on the side on which the artwork appears. Printers can also varnish the side of the schedule card containing the photo, but the cost of doing so is approximately the same as adding another color to the finished card. Another drawback is that coated papers are generally not recyclable.

ABOUT SELLING ADVERTISING

Regardless of the card style you choose, remember the general principle of printing multiple copies on a single sheet (see Figure 5.5), enabling you to recognize multiple advertisers and distribute costs among them.

Potential Costs

Using an 11- by 17-inch sheet, you can expect 5,000 all-sports pocket schedules run in a single color to cost approximately $500. Printing 5,000 single-sport schedule cards off the same sized sheet, printed in one color on both sides, would cost $350, and adding a second color to the front side would cost an additional $100. Prices will vary by printer and by changing conditions in the printing market, such as paper and ink costs.

Distribution and Quantities

Distribution points for pocket schedules are limited only by your imagination and community cooperation. Obvious options include displaying them in school main and athletic offices, and sending them to every parent. You should also check with high-traffic businesses in your community (e.g., gas stations, convenience stores, restaurants, banks, dry cleaners), and every advertiser is a natural distributor.

If you have no history of printing pocket schedules, estimating quantities is difficult. Typically, one in every eight people in your community will pick up a free schedule. You might adjust that ratio to 1:10 or higher if you have a lot of competition for attention.

199_ Schedule Pizza Shack 2525 W. Okemos	199_ Schedule Pizza Shack 2525 W. Okemos	199_ Schedule Pizza Shack 2525 W. Okemos	199_ Schedule Pizza Shack 2525 W. Okemos	199_ Schedule Pizza Shack 2525 W. Okemos	199_ Schedule Pizza Shack 2525 W. Okemos	199_ Schedule Pizza Shack 2525 W. Okemos	199_ Schedule Pizza Shack 2525 W. Okemos
199_ Schedule Elbinger Studios 555-5555	199_ Schedule Elbinger Studios 555-5555	199_ Schedule Elbinger Studios 555-5555	199_ Schedule Elbinger Studios 555-5555	199_ Schedule Elbinger Studios 555-5555	199_ Schedule Elbinger Studios 555-5555	199_ Schedule Elbinger Studios 555-5555	199_ Schedule Elbinger Studios 555-5555
199_ Schedule Farm Hill Insurance	199_ Schedule Farm Hill Insurance	199_ Schedule Farm Hill Insurance	199_ Schedule Farm Hill Insurance	199_ Schedule Farm Hill Insurance	199_ Schedule Farm Hill Insurance	199_ Schedule Farm Hill Insurance	199_ Schedule Farm Hill Insurance
199_ Schedule Student Book Store	199_ Schedule Student Book Store	199_ Schedule Student Book Store	199_ Schedule Student Book Store	199_ Schedule Student Book Store	199_ Schedule Student Book Store	199_ Schedule Student Book Store	199_ Schedule Student Book Store

Figure 5.5 Back of single-sport schedule card before cutting.

For example, in a high school of 1,000 students in a town of 40,000 people, you might print no more than 4,000 schedules—which still might be high. Remember that quantity of an all-sports pocket schedule is likely to be higher than a single-sport card because it appeals to a greater audience. When in doubt, print a lower quantity. You can always adjust totals season by season.

SCHEDULE POSTERS

Similar to pocket schedules, you can print schedule posters by season or sport, and some of the same principles apply. However, posters are not reference tools like pocket schedules. A poster generally has to tell its story in a few seconds as someone passes, but a well-made schedule poster can be an exception to this general rule. One of its primary purposes is to be referred to regularly.

All-Sports Poster

The all-sports poster can be published three times a year, containing all schedules, starting times, and names of head coaches. The poster can also contain a variety of action photographs, at least of varsity sports. Select high-quality photos: Too many posters are put out with fuzzy, out-of-focus photographs, adding nothing positive to the program.

These posters can be underwritten by a variety of sponsors. Frequently, posters include ads in columns on the right and left margins and across the bottom (see Figure 5.6).

Single-Sport Poster

The single-sport poster includes much of the same information found on the pocket schedule. The poster, however, may include a team photograph (sometimes in full color), as well as action shots. It too can have multiple sponsors. Some posters use a layout with pictures on the top, a schedule on the bottom (with blanks to fill in with scores), and advertisers in the middle, but your layout is up to you. A sample appears in Figure 5.7.

Sizes, Distribution, and Quantities

When printing such posters, you are again limited only by your imagination and sales ability. Sizes range from 11- by 17-inch sheets to about double that size, from one to four colors. Paper tends to be heavy, in the range of 80- to 100-pound stock. Posters that are folded for distribution by mail sometimes use 60-pound stock.

Estimate quantities of posters conservatively. If you've never produced a poster before, print one for each athlete on the poster, at least one for the primary businesses in your community, and at least six to put up in each building in your school district. You and your athletes can distribute the posters to businesses.

Poster Costs

Using a finished size of 17 by 22 inches, a two-color poster would cost approximately $500 for 500 pieces. The size of the sheet, number of colors, and quantity will influence the costs.

SELLING THE CONCEPT

Schedule cards and posters should be self-sufficient parts of your promotion program. Some people are willing to take a small loss, but your goal should be at least to break even. If you obtain sufficient sponsors, these promotions could become a modest revenue source.

If you have never produced schedule cards or posters before, you might first discuss the idea with key people within your organization and community to determine interest and potential advertising support. Just because others do so doesn't mean you need to or can!

Bids

Once you have determined your specifications, you should approach printers in your community, unless printing the job in-house is an option, and ask them to bid on the job. Check with your school district to determine its purchasing and bidding policies.

A poster like this can include all of the varsity schedules for all sports in a given season (fall, winter, or spring), or all levels of all sports in a season. The more schedules you include, the smaller the typesize will be and the fewer the ads. This sample shows only varsity sports.

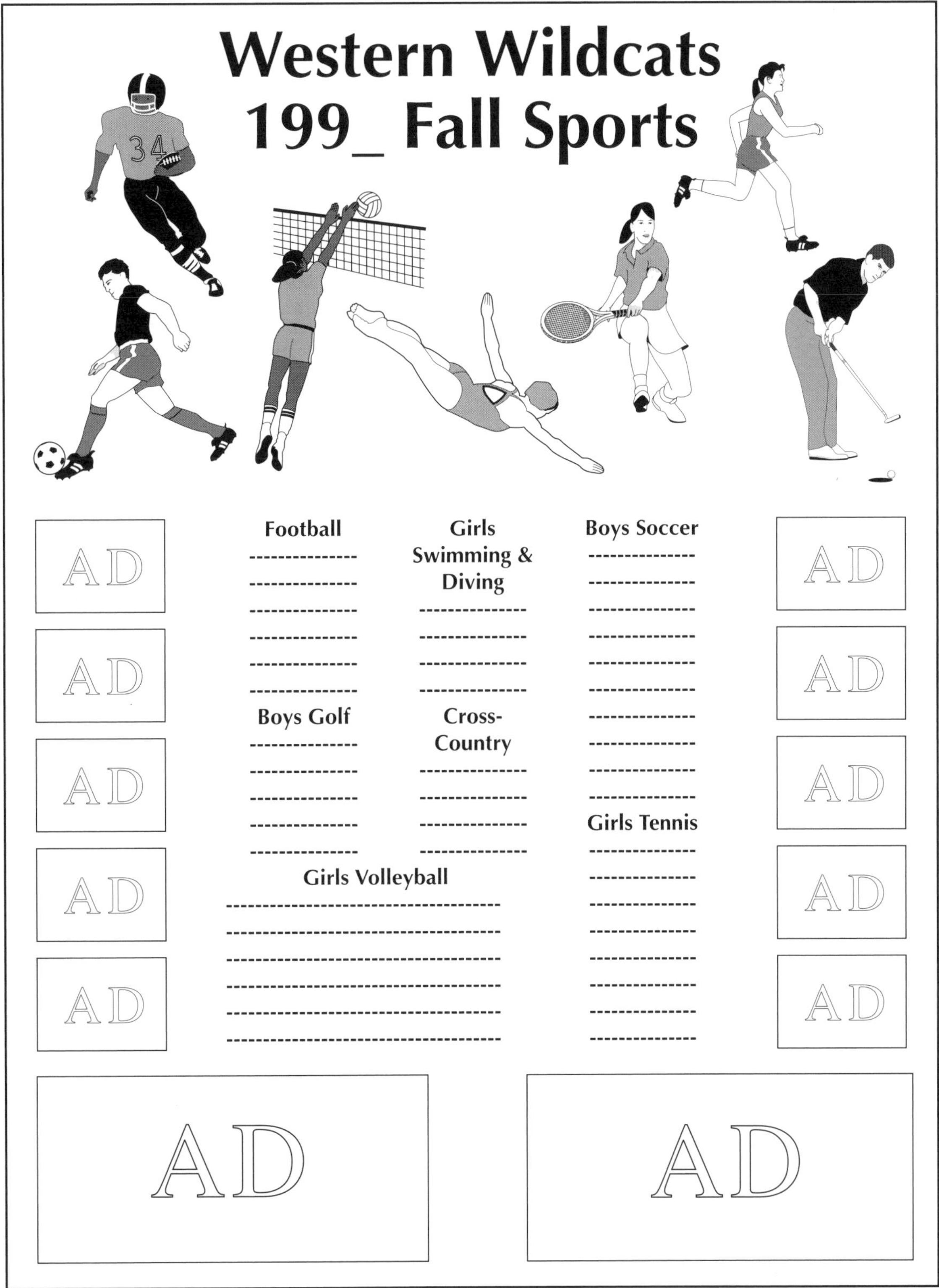

Figure 5.6 Sample all-sports poster.

A poster like this can include all of the schedules for the sport presented.

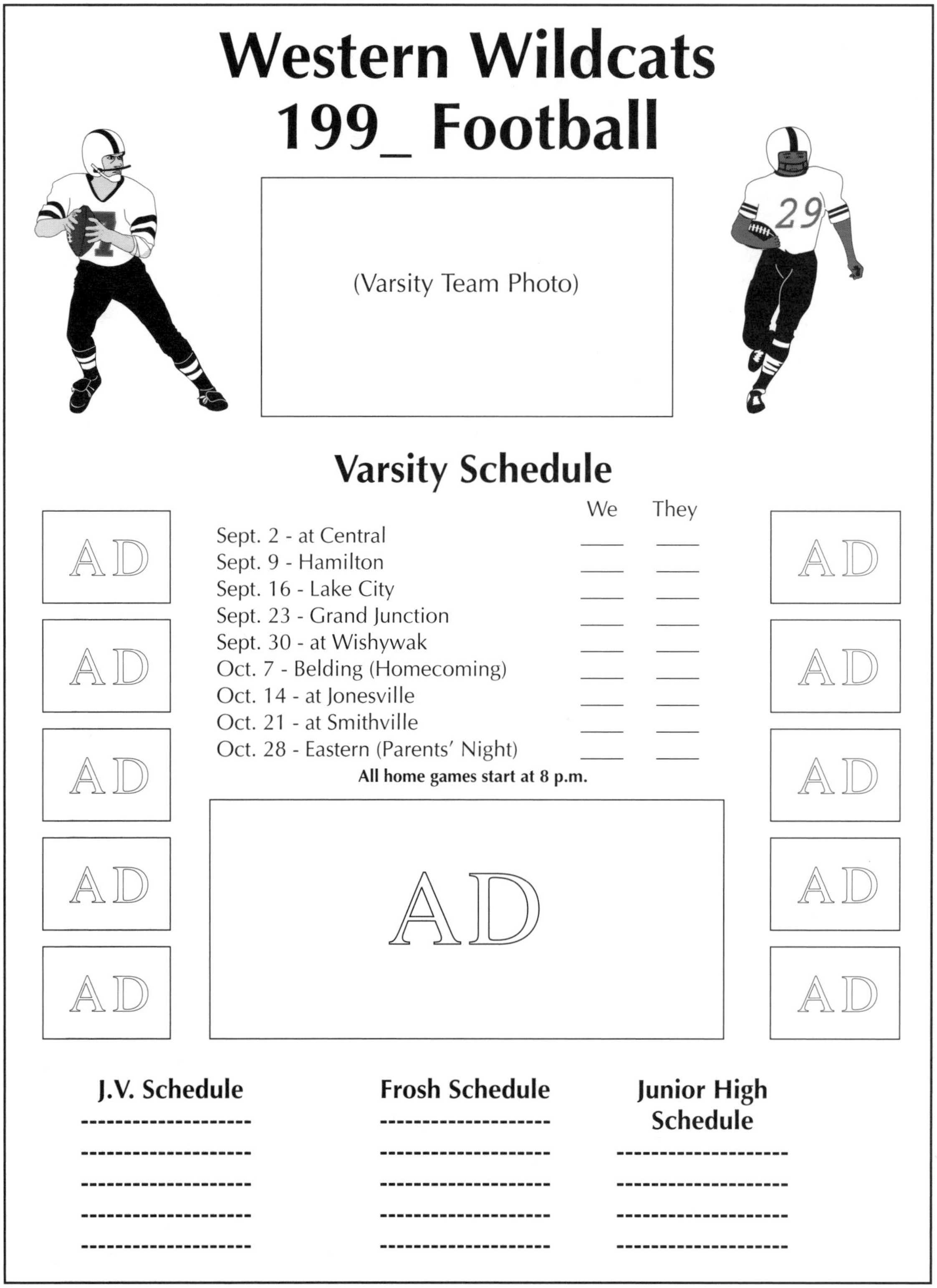

Western Wildcats
199_ Football

(Varsity Team Photo)

Varsity Schedule

	We	They
Sept. 2 - at Central	____	____
Sept. 9 - Hamilton	____	____
Sept. 16 - Lake City	____	____
Sept. 23 - Grand Junction	____	____
Sept. 30 - at Wishywak	____	____
Oct. 7 - Belding (Homecoming)	____	____
Oct. 14 - at Jonesville	____	____
Oct. 21 - at Smithville	____	____
Oct. 28 - Eastern (Parents' Night)	____	____

All home games start at 8 p.m.

AD AD AD AD AD

AD

AD AD AD AD AD

J.V. Schedule	**Frosh Schedule**	**Junior High Schedule**
--------------------	--------------------	--------------------
--------------------	--------------------	--------------------
--------------------	--------------------	--------------------
--------------------	--------------------	--------------------
--------------------	--------------------	

Figure 5.7 Sample single-sport poster.

When visiting a printer, bring an information sheet that will give the printer a general idea of what you want. If you've printed a similar job before, attach a copy of that card or poster to the bid specifications. To make accurate comparisons, you need all the printers to bid on the exact same specifications. You should encourage printers to offer you different options, but having everyone bid the job the same way is the most professional way to proceed. A sample bid spec sheet is shown in Figure 5.8. Also be sure that the printer understands that the job may not be printed if you cannot secure funding.

Advertising Rates

Once you know your printing price, you can determine how much to charge for advertising. Select from these approaches. First, you can try to split the ad costs evenly among the possible number of advertisers that can be involved, so that when you have sold every ad your costs are covered. Your second option is to figure that the break-even point is selling half to three-quarters of the available ad space, so that you make a modest profit for your program if you sell out. One way to reduce costs is to see if your printer will reduce your bill in trade for an ad on a schedule card or poster.

Consider a pocket schedule card as an example. If the printer charges you $500 for 5,000 units, and you can accommodate up to five sponsors, you could either charge $100 per advertiser, requiring five ads to break even, or charge $125 or $175 per advertiser, so the break-even point would be achieved with the third or fourth ad, and a sellout would net your program additional revenue.

If your school district is fortunate enough to have the capabilities, you should also consider internal printing options. Many graphic arts and printing classes welcome the opportunity to work with jobs such as these. Because your costs may be limited to materials, you might either charge less for ads or realize a significant profit by charging the rates you would use if the job were being printed commercially.

One issue you should address with your business office or organization auditors is how to handle money you generate beyond the actual cost of printing. The Internal Revenue Service regulates unrelated business income for nonprofit organizations. Since most schools are nonprofit entities, this additional income might be subject to taxes.

Your High School
199_ Football Schedule Card
Bidding Specifications

Quantity:	10,000
Trim size:	2 1/4 × 3 3/8
Paper stock:	100-pound cover, coated on one side
Halftones:	One on front
Reverses:	One on front
Text:	Schedule on back, hard copy. Ads to be provided camera ready.
Delivery:	July 15 to Your High School athletics
Notes:	There are four advertisers. Strip ads so an equal number of cards are allotted to each advertiser.
Submit bids by:	June 1
Bid awarded by:	June 15
For more information contact:	Joe Dokes, Athletic Director, Your High School, 555-5555

Figure 5.8 Schedule card bidding specifications sheet.

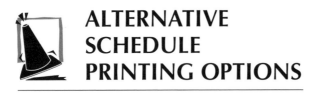

ALTERNATIVE SCHEDULE PRINTING OPTIONS

Some companies will print pocket schedules and posters for free if they retain the advertising revenues. It puts such a vendor at risk, but reduces your role to gathering the information and photographs to be included on the schedule card or poster, and informing your community that an outside firm will be soliciting the ads for this printing job.

These companies tend to focus more on schedule posters than cards because posters offer so many more opportunities for involving advertisers. Before signing with any such company, get a list of references of schools it has worked with before and samples of finished products. And don't let them tell you they aren't making money on your job—they wouldn't do it if they couldn't make any money!

In some communities, soft drink or snack companies can make available generic poster stock that they will print your schedule on. It may not be the best option available, but it is one way to get your message out and possibly a means of striking up a relationship with a vendor you might be able to call on at a later date.

GAME PROGRAMS

Souvenir game programs may not be your most important responsibility, but they can be one of the most visible. They certainly paint a picture of how the school athletic program is perceived in the community. A program is also one of a young person's most tangible reminders of involvement in interscholastic athletics. Scrapbooks across the country are filled with old programs. The opportunity for athletes to have a name, a picture, or anything in print about them is invaluable to their self-esteem.

Carefully planned, game programs can also be a source of revenue for your program. It's not easy, but if you're willing to balance text and other elements with advertising revenue, or find an alternative method of getting the program produced, you can make programs quite profitable. Producing programs can involve other students in your school. A graphics arts, printing, or journalism class can be responsible for a portion of the work, cutting down your involvement and costs.

The rest of this chapter examines the different aspects of the souvenir game program and how you can best suit them to your situation.

Selecting a Program Type

The kind of program you produce will depend on your organizational philosophy and how it relates to specific sports. Among the questions you should ask are these:

- How much time do we have to put a program together?
- Are there resources available to accomplish this project?
- How big of a demand is there for a particular sport or event program?

If You Lack Time or Resources

A school that lacks umbrella or individual sport booster clubs (you are better off with an umbrella booster club), or where the athletic department staff lacks release time to solicit advertising should consider three basic kinds of game programs:

- A single sheet of paper with the rosters of each team on each side
- An 11- by 17-inch sheet of paper folded in half to create a four-page program (an 8 1/2- by 11-inch sheet, once folded, reduces the information to a size that is hard to read and looks downright cheap)
- Partially preprinted program paper stock. This form includes areas for you to imprint rosters on one side of the sheet, and other brief game-related information on the side that serves as the cover. This used to be a very popular program for schools, and soft drink companies provided the preprinted four-color stock. This program still appears in some communities, although the trend has gone away from generic designs toward designs that are more school specific.

If You Have the Means

A school with additional resources can pursue a magazine-style program with a four-page center section that changes for each event. This can be sport or season specific. You should have the center section stitched into the book; it looks cheap to have something inserted into a good-looking book that can fall out when you open it.

These programs tend to be printed for fall and winter sports, when attendance is higher than in the spring. They usually include pictures and schedules of all the teams from that season. If left up to individual sport coaches, parents, or booster clubs, quality will vary from sport to sport, and the program may not include all the young people involved in that sport. Again, individual efforts may pit sports against one another in your building and your community, which harms everyone in the long run.

What To Put in Your Game Program

Many traditionalists want the program to include just the date of the game, the site, the name of the opponent, and the rosters of both teams. It is the most basic information and is really the heart of a good program. It is up to you if you want to take your program to a higher level (e.g., include team pictures, season schedules and results, feature stories, etc.) to better promote your school and its students.

Rosters

A good program roster should be in numerical order, with information columns as follow: (a) number, (b) first and last name, (c) position(s), (d) height, (e) weight, and (f) class. A sample was shown in chapter 4 in the section on public relations (see Figure 4.5, p. 45). Programs for sports that use numbers on the game uniform should list them numerically, beginning with 0 or 1, making it easier for readers to associate players' names with their numbers.

If any numbers vary on home and away uniforms, produce separate columns for numbers, listing players by their home uniform numbers. A good roster also shows how many varsity letters a player has won in the sport. This is best accomplished with asterisks immediately preceding or following each player's name.

For sports such as wrestling, where numbers are not used, listing by weight class in alphabetical order works well. Other sports, such as gymnastics, track and field, and swimming and diving, can only list players alphabetically.

At the bottom of the roster, it is helpful to include the following names: head coach, assistant coaches, managers, trainers, and cheerleaders. This is important even if you are producing the most basic of programs. It recognizes the primary people involved on the team.

Schedule

Next in importance would be including a team schedule. As previously discussed, dates, sites, and starting times are essential items. You cannot assume the person picking up the program already has a copy of the schedule in some other form. A sample schedule appears in chapter 4 (see Figure 4.4, p. 45). The more ways you can use to communicate your schedule, the more you increase attendance. That is why having sub-varsity schedules in varsity souvenir programs is worth considering. Including lower-profile sport schedules in a football or basketball program helps.

Other Information

If you can include more information in your program, we offer a few ideas for popular material to include:

- Team pictures. Include a picture of your team, and if the format of your program allows and your opponent can provide it, a picture of the visiting team. If the program serves as an all-sports program for a season, include pictures of all teams at all levels.
- Cheerleader pictures. Many schools recognize their cheerleading squads by placing their group picture in programs.
- Support staff and group pictures. Include pictures of the coaching staff, school administration, trainers and managers, marching band, and other groups involved in games.
- Pictures of individual players. In addition to the team photo, including individual head shots of players is a very nice touch. Sometimes, mug shots may be limited to seniors in a single-sport program. We don't recommend it for an all-sports program—it is cost prohibitive.
- Letters of welcome. These letters can come from the superintendent, athletic director,

principal, or coach. They help set the tone for the event. You need not have a letter from each. One letter of welcome, bearing the names of all parties, provides a valuable opportunity to deliver a message to your spectators about the value of the athletic program, sportsmanship, and your appreciation of fans' support.

- Scorecards. Particularly in basketball, people like to track how many points and fouls players accumulate as the game progresses. The best basketball scorecard in a program is one that includes numbers for readers to cross out as the game progresses. Spectators can look down and tally baskets, free throws, and fouls at a glance (see Figure 5.9). You can also use this method to create scorecards for hockey, baseball, and softball very easily.
- Stadium and school information. A few quick facts about the facility can familiarize spectators with the locations of first aid stations and restroom facilities, as well as the history of the facility. This information could also serve as another recognition tool for a historic figure or for those who helped make the facility a reality. Other items, such as record attendance at the facility, the school's win-loss record since beginning play at the facility, and records set at the facility also make enjoyable reading for spectators.
- All-sports schedules. The program is a good place to get the word out about sport

Player	Field goals	Free throws	Fouls	FG	FT	TP
	2 2 2 2 2 2 2 2 2 2 2 3 3 3 3 3	1 1 1 1 1 1 1 1 1 1 1 1	1 2 3 4 5			
	2 2 2 2 2 2 2 2 2 2 2 3 3 3 3 3	1 1 1 1 1 1 1 1 1 1 1 1	1 2 3 4 5			
	2 2 2 2 2 2 2 2 2 2 2 3 3 3 3 3	1 1 1 1 1 1 1 1 1 1 1 1	1 2 3 4 5			
	2 2 2 2 2 2 2 2 2 2 2 3 3 3 3 3	1 1 1 1 1 1 1 1 1 1 1 1	1 2 3 4 5			
	2 2 2 2 2 2 2 2 2 2 2 3 3 3 3 3	1 1 1 1 1 1 1 1 1 1 1 1	1 2 3 4 5			
	2 2 2 2 2 2 2 2 2 2 2 3 3 3 3 3	1 1 1 1 1 1 1 1 1 1 1 1	1 2 3 4 5			
	2 2 2 2 2 2 2 2 2 2 2 3 3 3 3 3	1 1 1 1 1 1 1 1 1 1 1 1	1 2 3 4 5			
	2 2 2 2 2 2 2 2 2 2 2 3 3 3 3 3	1 1 1 1 1 1 1 1 1 1 1 1	1 2 3 4 5			
	2 2 2 2 2 2 2 2 2 2 2 3 3 3 3 3	1 1 1 1 1 1 1 1 1 1 1 1	1 2 3 4 5			
	2 2 2 2 2 2 2 2 2 2 2 3 3 3 3 3	1 1 1 1 1 1 1 1 1 1 1 1	1 2 3 4 5			
	2 2 2 2 2 2 2 2 2 2 2 3 3 3 3 3	1 1 1 1 1 1 1 1 1 1 1 1	1 2 3 4 5			
	2 2 2 2 2 2 2 2 2 2 2 3 3 3 3 3	1 1 1 1 1 1 1 1 1 1 1 1	1 2 3 4 5			
	2 2 2 2 2 2 2 2 2 2 2 3 3 3 3 3	1 1 1 1 1 1 1 1 1 1 1 1	1 2 3 4 5			
	2 2 2 2 2 2 2 2 2 2 2 3 3 3 3 3	1 1 1 1 1 1 1 1 1 1 1 1	1 2 3 4 5			

Player	Field goals	Free throws	Fouls	FG	FT	TP
	2 2 2 2 2 2 2 2 2 2 2 3 3 3 3 3	1 1 1 1 1 1 1 1 1 1 1 1	1 2 3 4 5			
	2 2 2 2 2 2 2 2 2 2 2 3 3 3 3 3	1 1 1 1 1 1 1 1 1 1 1 1	1 2 3 4 5			
	2 2 2 2 2 2 2 2 2 2 2 3 3 3 3 3	1 1 1 1 1 1 1 1 1 1 1 1	1 2 3 4 5			
	2 2 2 2 2 2 2 2 2 2 2 3 3 3 3 3	1 1 1 1 1 1 1 1 1 1 1 1	1 2 3 4 5			
	2 2 2 2 2 2 2 2 2 2 2 3 3 3 3 3	1 1 1 1 1 1 1 1 1 1 1 1	1 2 3 4 5			
	2 2 2 2 2 2 2 2 2 2 2 3 3 3 3 3	1 1 1 1 1 1 1 1 1 1 1 1	1 2 3 4 5			
	2 2 2 2 2 2 2 2 2 2 2 3 3 3 3 3	1 1 1 1 1 1 1 1 1 1 1 1	1 2 3 4 5			
	2 2 2 2 2 2 2 2 2 2 2 3 3 3 3 3	1 1 1 1 1 1 1 1 1 1 1 1	1 2 3 4 5			
	2 2 2 2 2 2 2 2 2 2 2 3 3 3 3 3	1 1 1 1 1 1 1 1 1 1 1 1	1 2 3 4 5			
	2 2 2 2 2 2 2 2 2 2 2 3 3 3 3 3	1 1 1 1 1 1 1 1 1 1 1 1	1 2 3 4 5			
	2 2 2 2 2 2 2 2 2 2 2 3 3 3 3 3	1 1 1 1 1 1 1 1 1 1 1 1	1 2 3 4 5			
	2 2 2 2 2 2 2 2 2 2 2 3 3 3 3 3	1 1 1 1 1 1 1 1 1 1 1 1	1 2 3 4 5			
	2 2 2 2 2 2 2 2 2 2 2 3 3 3 3 3	1 1 1 1 1 1 1 1 1 1 1 1	1 2 3 4 5			
	2 2 2 2 2 2 2 2 2 2 2 3 3 3 3 3	1 1 1 1 1 1 1 1 1 1 1 1	1 2 3 4 5			

Figure 5.9 Scorecard.

schedules, not only for teams the program is being produced for, but also for other teams and co-curricular events.

- Special articles. You can use feature articles to promote values such as sportsmanship, as well as other school activities. You may generate copy through journalism classes, reprints of articles from local newspapers, or camera-ready slicks that are available from athletic governing bodies. It is helpful, but expensive, to change these articles regularly, but they add a nice touch to the publication.
- School records. If you keep good records for each team, printing information about individual play, single-game, single-season, or career records provides additional recognition for the achievements of former players.

This list could go on and on, and your program could start to resemble or even become superior to some collegiate programs. We've started you out with what we feel to be the necessities. If you want some ideas for how these items are laid out, collect old programs from other high school, college, and professional games. And don't feel bad about *stealing* an idea you see in another program. Athletic publicists have long felt that imitation is the highest form of compliment in the program business.

Tips on Photographs

The best way to ensure that you can get all your team pictures done consistently is to schedule one day when all the team photographs for that season will be taken. Some teams may have to give up a portion of a practice day, but this approach reduces anxiety in the person assembling the program, allows you to use one photographer (preferably your yearbook or other professional photographer), and promotes consistency in presentation among teams. Here are some other notes:

- Be sure the team pictures are taken with a high-quality camera (35mm or larger format with adjustable focus and lighting).
- Shoot the picture in two or more horizontal rows, making every effort to fill the viewfinder with the team members from top to bottom and side to side.
- Avoid team pictures using two long horizontal rows, vertical formations, or cute photos like a school block letter or assembling on a ladder, tank, or car. To make these photos fit, pictures have to be cropped and faces wind up being smaller.
- Be sure the background provides enough contrast so players' faces can be seen.
- Before the group breaks up after the photo, identify all individuals and their positions in the picture.

Flipping Out

While we like to think all our athletes are solid in character, a couple of group photo stories remind us that kids will be kids.

While preparing a program for the football state finals, the editor noticed someone sitting cross legged in the front row with his arms between his legs and his right hand turned up, his middle finger stuck clearly in the air (not to signal that his team was number one!). A little creativity with an eraser and some paper correction fluid took care of that problem. Today, the process could be even easier and the results cleaner looking if the photo is scanned into a computer file, then touched up with an art or drawing program.

A newspaper, however, wasn't so lucky as it gathered an all-area volleyball team. Several girls in the front row *flipped off* the camera during one of the shots, thinking the photograph would never be used. After a pose was selected, a print was made, and it passed through the sports department, the layout department, the camera and stripping department, then on to the press.

The photo appearing in the Sunday sports section was the shot in which the entire front row flipped off the camera. In addition to the natural embarrassment to the newspaper, schools, and athletes involved, a couple of local businesses which had previously sponsored a large invitational tournament that past season withdrew their future support.

Sample Layouts

If you decide to develop a program that goes beyond printing rosters on both sides of a single sheet of paper, you need to plan how to arrange information inside your program.

Fours and Eights

A basic printing premise is that you plan your book in multiples of four or eight pages, depending on how large a sheet of paper you will be printing on. Some printers have large enough presses to print 16 pages at a time. Here, we discuss layouts of 4-, 8-, 16-, 24-, and 32-page programs, working in multiples of four and eight pages, and assuming that the publication is a *self-cover* (meaning that a separate, four-page cover is not being printed in addition to the text). If necessary, you can adjust these grids to include a cover.

The Four-Page Program

This is a good approach for a single-game or event publication. A *signature* (layout) sheet is shown in Figure 5.10. Although you can only include the most basic information, you can make an attractive, potential revenue-producing program.

You can print the outside portion of the sheet (pages 1 and 4) for the entire season at one time, which might allow you to use more than one color. This cover design could also enable your printer to come back and imprint the name of the opponent and date of the game for each contest on the front. A sample appears in Figure 5.11. Game information could go on the inside, but the advantage of imprinting it on the outside is that, as the season progresses, you can easily distinguish among different game programs in your files. The back cover could include either an advertisement or a combination of a season schedule, picture of the varsity team, and an advertisement.

On the inside, you should include varsity and junior varsity rosters for your teams and those of the visiting school, perhaps including scorecards for each on facing pages. You could also leave out scorecards, allowing additional space for advertisements, a welcome letter, or some other message from the school.

The Eight-Page Program

Shown in Figure 5.12, the eight-page program is an extension of the four-page program, adding flexibility. Using the two signature sheets shown, this program could be printed on two 11- by 17-inch sheets, or on a sheet allowing all eight pages to be printed at one time.

If printing two 11- by 17-inch sheets, the first signature could be the outer section, printed for the entire season, potentially in more than one color (at least on the front and back cover positions). Welcome messages, schedules, and team photos could be printed on the inside cover positions, and there would be ample advertising opportunities.

The second 11- by 17-inch sheet would include the rosters for your school and the visiting team on the center spread (pages 4 and 5), and pages 3 and 6 could be printed for the season (with information like pictures of cheerleaders and reserve teams), or could be printed for that game, promoting special occasions like homecoming or senior night.

Larger Programs

When you develop 16-, 24-, and 32-page or larger programs, you can include all levels of one sport, the varsity levels of all sports for that season, or all sports at all levels for a single season. Sample signature sheets are shown in appendix A.

An important point to remember, however, is that unless you devise an alternative method to fund the program, you need to develop an advertising to editorial copy mix that will fund at least a portion of the book. You will notice that every signature sheet shown here has a 50/50 mix of advertising to editorial copy, an approach explained later in this chapter.

How to Get Students Involved

Involving students in the production of game programs is as important as organizing spirit clubs, booster club workers, and volunteers for other auxiliary services. The most logical sources are journalism, printing, and art classes, as well as individuals from the school newspaper or yearbook.

Many schools have computers with some kind of graphics or desktop publishing capabilities and classes being taught in those areas, providing you a

This program is set up on an 11- by 17-inch sheet of paper. The pages in the top row (4 and 1) will be printed on one side of the sheet, the pages in the bottom row (2 and 3) on the other. When finished and folded, the pages read sequentially. Here is a mock-up of a four-page program. The streamer ads are shown in the layout as ads that run across the bottom of a page.

Page 1 - Cover/streamer ad

Page 4 - Team picture/schedule/ streamer ad

Page 2 - Varsity rosters/scorecard/ streamer ad

Page 3 - Junior varsity rosters/scorecard/ streamer ad

Page 4

Meet The Wildcats

Team Photo Here

199_ Schedule

Al's Body Shop
222 N. Centre Road

Page 1

Jason High School
199_ Girls Basketball

vs. Kokomo
Jan. 15 • Souvenir Program

Joe's Pizza
555-5555

Page 2

Varsity Rosters

Jason Kokomo

Scorecard

McGuire's Restaurant
US 2 & Miller Road

Page 3

J.V. Rosters

Jason Kokomo

Scorecard

The Sports Section
Downtown Ashton

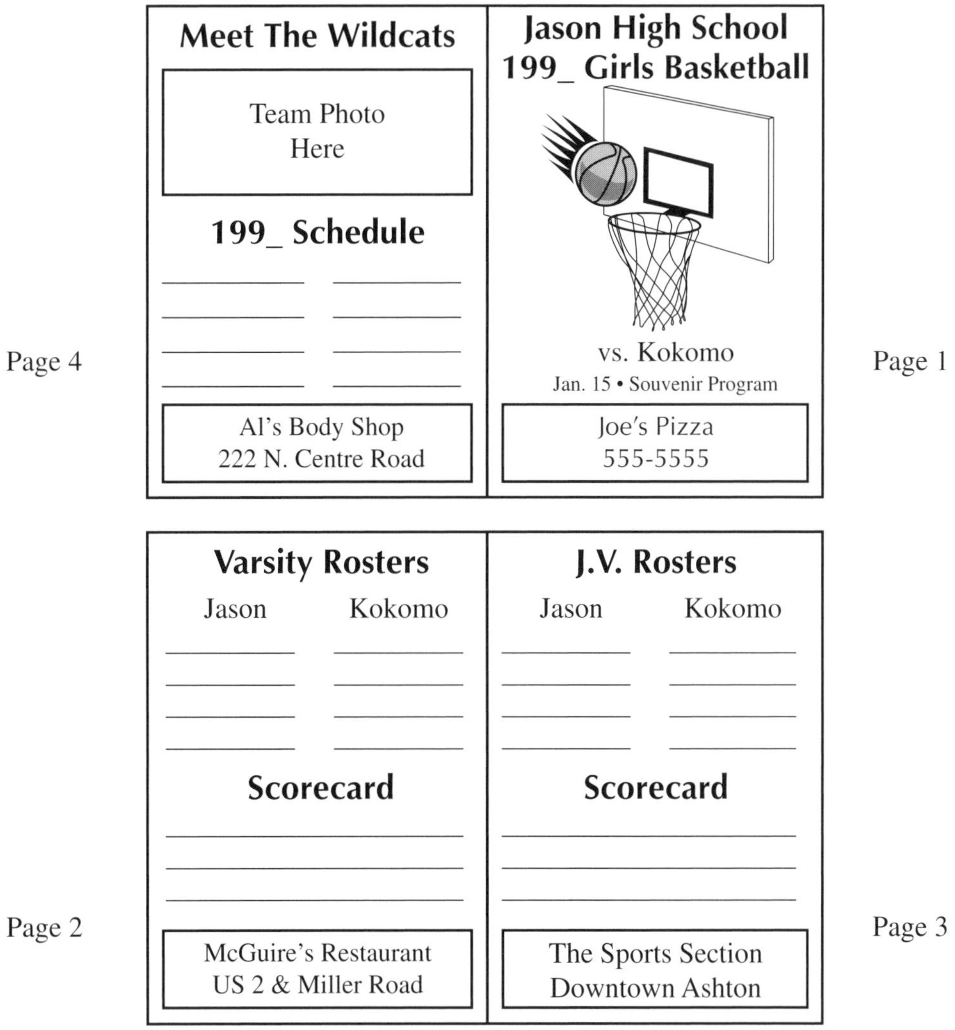

Figure 5.10 Four-page program signature.

This represents the front and back covers of the program, which could be preprinted for the entire season. Information that changes with each game can be printed on the other side. You could print the cover in two to four colors of ink. The imprint of the specific game could be imprinted for each contest.

Back Cover *Front Cover*

Figure 5.11 Cover design of a four-page program.

source for producing a program of the quality you will want to display in the community, as well as more student involvement.

These students can write stories or take pictures for the programs. They should be the most advanced students available, and be supervised by a teacher or advisor you can designate. Students have also long assumed the responsibility for selling ads in school yearbooks and newspapers, and they could use these skills for your program. Consider carefully, however, that you may already be contacting businesses in your community for other kinds of monetary support.

Printing Options

Similar to previous discussions of schedule cards and posters, you have a variety of printing options at your disposal for producing game programs. Options again include what you can produce in-house, using a commercial printer, or contracting the services of a publisher that handles all elements of your program and delivers to you at no cost, so that you can make money off the actual sale of the publication.

In-House Printing

One of your best options for printing is the in-house method of producing a program on existing school equipment, ranging from programs coming off the photocopier or stencil machine to an offset printing job if you have the capabilities. The in-house option is likely to be the most economical, especially if it can be done as a class project.

The in-house project could involve other students in the actual design and typesetting of the program, as well as with photography. Many of the word processing programs available on computers today are capable of low-end desktop publishing work. Having a laser printer available to print the original

This program is set up using two 11- by 17-inch sheets of paper. The pages in the top row of each signature (8 and 1, 6 and 3) will be printed on one side of the sheet, the pages in the bottom row of each signature (2 and 7, 4 and 5) on the other. When finished and folded, the pages read sequentially. Here is a mock-up of an eight-page program. The streamer ads referred to below are shown in the layout as ads that run across the bottom of a page.

(First signature is printed for entire season.)

Page 1 - Cover/streamer ad	Page 2 - Letters of welcome
Page 8 - Ad	Page 7 - Team and cheerleader pictures/streamer ad

---

(Second signature is printed game by game.)

Page 3 - Tonight's game/half-page ad	Page 4 - Varsity rosters/scorecard/streamer ad
Page 6 - Schedule and results/streamer ad	Page 5 - Junior varsity rosters/scorecard/streamer ad

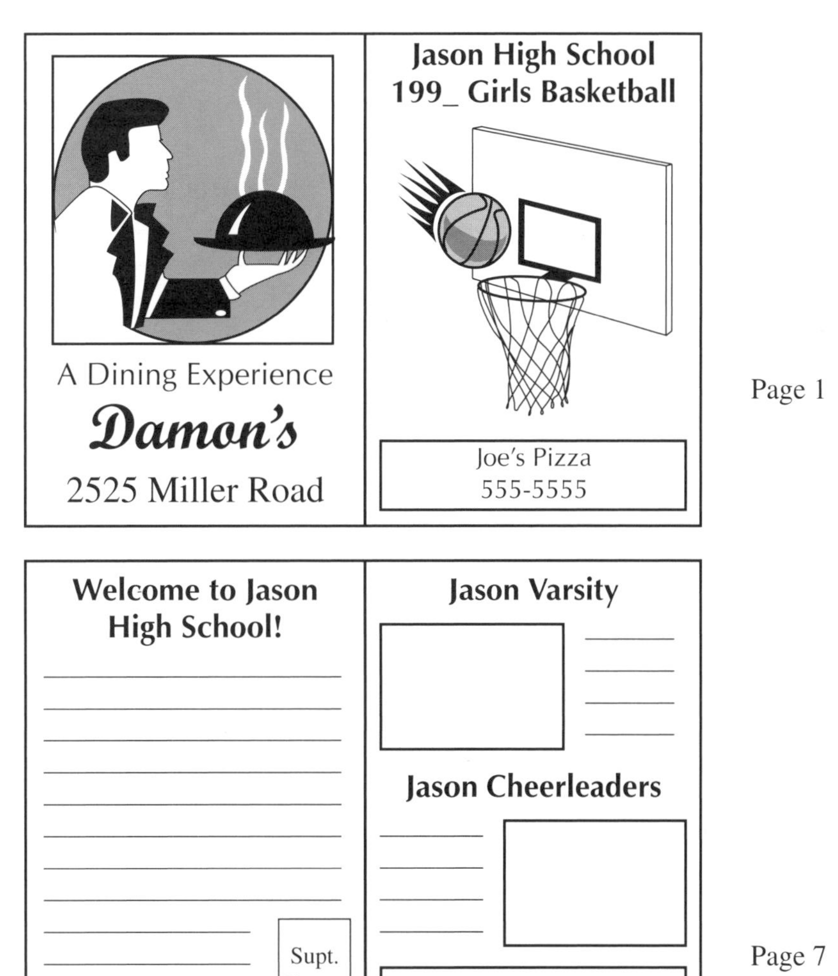

(continued)

Figure 5.12 Eight-page program signature.

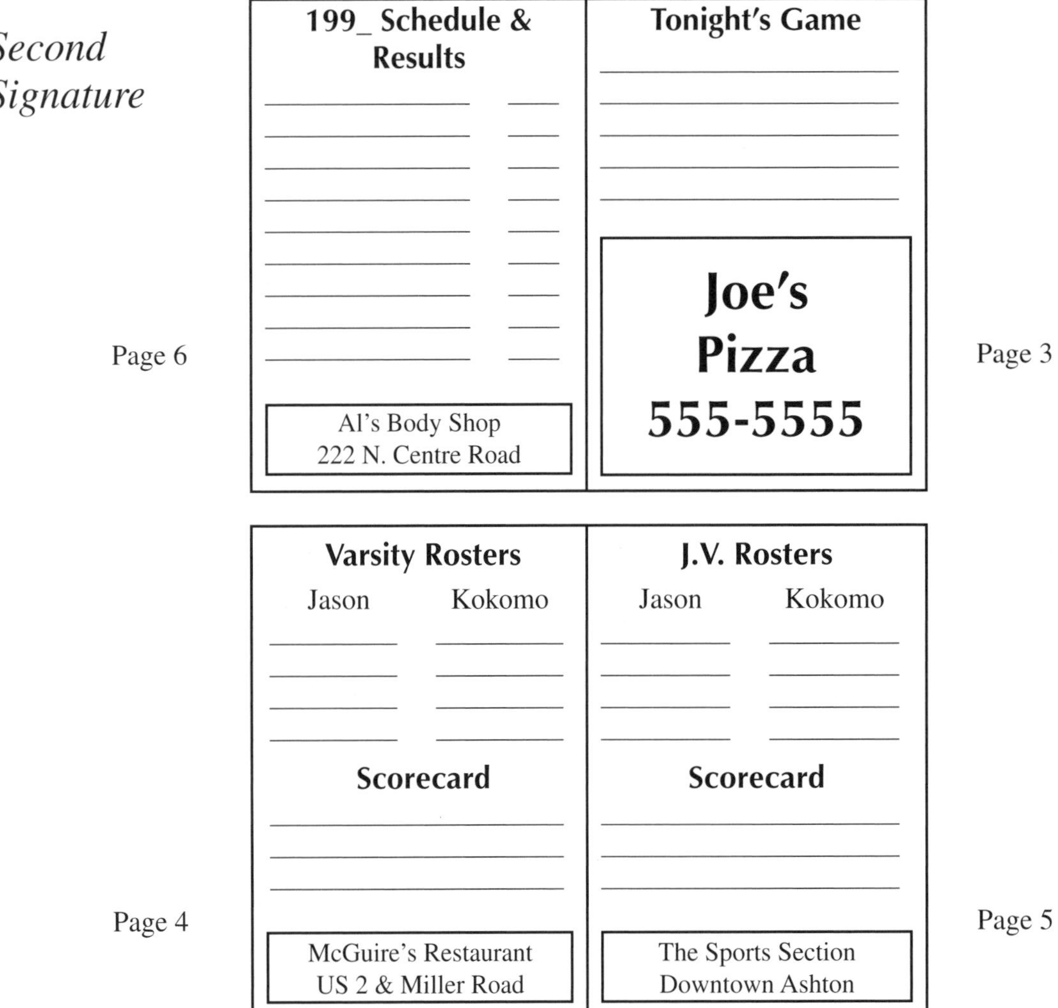

Figure 5.12 *(continued)*

pages before they are shot for the presses would enhance the look of your in-house production.

Commercial Printers

Your options for commercial printing include a standard offset printing house or one of the many *quick print* shops that have flourished around the country in the past decade. Many printers still offer a full line of services, including typesetting and design, to assist you. If you have the capability at your school to produce camera-ready pages off a laser printer, you may save some money by eliminating that part of the job at your printer. Select printers carefully. Some may offer a price break for using cheap printing plates, but the quality of the book may diminish.

Desktop Publishing Notes

With the advancements in desktop publishing, some printers avoid the traditional method of having a camera shoot all the pictures to be included in the program by scanning photos into a computer. Don't be your printer's guinea pig if it is just beginning to offer this service to customers. If you are producing the program in-house and scanning photos is an option, you have to make a decision if you are intent on giving the kids in the print shop that opportunity. Printers usually take some time to perfect their scanning of photographs and getting them to reproduce with the same quality as using a camera to shoot the pictures.

Program Printing Companies

An alternative to doing all this work yourself can take the guesswork out of parts of the process. There may be a printing company in your area which specializes in producing game programs. These companies generally get the copy from you, then handle the ad sales and absorb the printing costs. You are given a program at no cost which you may distribute as you see fit. If you decide to sell the programs, your organization will realize a profit from the first program sold and incur no financial risk.

Remember, however, that these companies are for-profit corporations, and their ad rates may be higher than what you would charge. Also, these people may do your program one year and not come back if they weren't able to sell the necessary advertising.

There is another risk that accompanies having a private company represent your organization in a sales role in your community. Most program publishing companies sell advertising exclusively by telephone, eliminating personal contact with potential advertisers. Some people in your community may find this kind of contact offensive because they have never had personal contact with the voice at the other end of the phone, or because they dislike telephone solicitation in general. The positive side to this approach is that the risk factor of selling advertising and the legwork that goes with producing a program is taken away from you. You will obtain a program at least once, regardless of how many ads the company sells in your community.

Determining Costs—Getting Bids

You've established what you want in the program, laid it out, and determined how many pages the editorial portion of the book will take. Now multiply that by two—figuring that half of your game program is devoted to advertising—and you've established how many pages your book can be.

After you have done a *mock-up* of the book (roughed out on a signature sheet what will appear on each page), seek bids from two to four printers, so you will know what it will cost to produce the book for the season. Be sure you figure advertising into the mix (see pp. 86–87 for a formula for determining quantities). Also be careful with the number of pictures in the book, which can drive the cost up.

When you visit printers to seek bids for the book, be sure you are specific about every aspect of the book:

- Printing quantity
- Number of pages
- Weight of the paper
- Number of colors of ink (black plus any additional colors)
- Number of pictures
- Timetable for copy being delivered to the printer and amount of typesetting required
- Timetable for advertisements being delivered to the printer and amount of typesetting and design required
- Expected delivery date of the finished publication

The bidding process should take place at least 3 months before you begin submitting copy to the printer selected for the job. Make sure when securing a bid that the price quoted will be good for that school year (e.g., if bidding your winter sports program during the summer). With changing economic conditions, some printers will only guarantee a price for so many days. Make sure you are locked in at that price, provided you make no major changes once you begin the project. A sample bid sheet appears in Figure 5.13.

The bid sheet will determine the base price. Find out from each printer whether their price includes typesetting corrections before the final proof. If corrections are not included in the bid, count on paying between $25 and $30 per hour for typesetting corrections. Some typesetters charge by the page for excessive corrections at about half of their hourly rate. The typesetting corrections will be based on how many corrections *you* make on the proofs. The only way to keep corrections to a minimum is to give your printer the most complete information the first time. One final matter to explore with your printer is whether a discount will be extended if you include an ad for the printer in the program.

Your High School
199_ Boys Basketball Program
Bidding Specifications

Quantity:	Vary by game — see schedule below
Trim size:	8 1/2 × 11
Paper stock:	60-pound text
Number of pages:	8, self-cover
Colors:	First signature prints two colors on one side, black and white one side. Second signature prints black and white both sides. Second color is red (PMS 185).
Halftones:	3
Reverses and screens:	6 total
Text:	All hard copy. Ads to be provided camera ready.
Notes:	First signature is printed for entire season. Second signature prints game by game. Copy to be submitted 1 week prior to delivery date. Layout for second signature to stay same for all games. Sample of last year's program attached.
Submit bids by:	June 1
Bid awarded by:	June 15

Delivery schedule with quantities — delivery to Gannon Gymnasium

Dec. 1	Gas City	500
Dec. 8	Wachovia	750
Dec. 20	Bloomington	400
Jan. 10	Monroesville	500
Jan. 17	Belleville	500
Jan. 30	Buggsville	750
Feb. 7	Bakersfield Central	400
Feb. 14	Millersburg	750
Feb. 22	Mount Forester	1,000

For more information contact: Joe Dokes, Athletic Director, Your High School, 555-5555

Figure 5.13 Program bidding specifications sheet.

How Many to Print and Whom to Comp

In general, spectators buying programs at high school games buy at a 1:6 to 1:8 ratio. That is, one program is purchased for every six to eight fans in attendance.

- If your gym holds 2,400 people and you're expecting to sell out for that game, printing somewhere between 300 and 400 programs is generally a good figure to work with. This figure could vary, depending on your sales price, and some experimenting may be required.
- If you're giving the program away, a 1:2 to 1:4 ratio will work best. In that same sold-out 2,400-seat gym, you would need to print 600 to 1,200 programs per game.
- Don't overestimate your sales potential—too many sport directors do. Even major college football bowl games have a hard time reaching a 1:3 or 1:2 ratio.
- It's better to run out of programs than to have several boxes left over.
- Always provide complimentary programs to the media, and consider providing programs gratis for the visiting team and game officials.

It is a matter of courtesy to do so. However, when comping a team, especially those with large numbers, remember that quite a bit of money could be going out in good will.

- An alternative may be to provide comps to the visiting team at the end of the game if a surplus of programs is available.

Getting Your Program Paid for—Advertising

Unless you can absorb costs for producing programs internally, soliciting advertising is a necessary step in producing game programs. Besides helping you to fund the program, they also give community individuals and businesses an opportunity to visibly support area schools and athletic teams.

Your goal for advertising is at least to pay for the book before you print it. This theory assumes you'll cover all production costs up front, then profit from the sales of programs at games. (If you're not seeking income, then you get the costs covered up front so you can give the programs away.)

A basic souvenir program should strive for a 50 percent editorial to 50 percent advertising mix. Your community makeup will help dictate how close you can come to hitting that blend. A school in a community with many businesses has more potential advertisers than a rural community where the major industry may be agriculture.

Once you have determined the cost to produce the program for the season, divide that cost by the number of pages you will print for the entire season (*not* a single game). For example, if the cost to produce your program for the season is $2,400, and there are 24 pages in a book each game, your cost to produce a single page is $100. Assuming a 50/50 mix of editorial copy and advertising, that figure of $100 becomes the cost of a half-page ad (50 percent of the page).

This formula comes from Tom Lamonica, the sports information director at Illinois State University, and there probably isn't a better method for determining advertising rates. If you hit that 50/50 mix, your book will be paid for in advertising, and sales are pure profit for your program.

Figure 5.14 provides an illustration of what different sized advertisements could cost, using the 50/50 advertising to editorial mix, and the cost per page for a season of $100, the cost for a half-page ad.

Adjust that half-page figure slightly up or down for a larger or smaller ad. For a full page, multiply the $100 by 2.1 to determine the full-page ad rate of $210. For a quarter page, multiply the $100 by .6 to get an ad rate of $60. An eighth-page ad would sell at .4 of the half-page rate: $40. In addition, the booster ad, a one- or two-line listing of an individual's name or name of a business, is a popular way to involve parties that could not otherwise

This formula is courtesy of Tom Lamonica, the sports information director at Illinois State University. All of the ad rates shown assume your program will have a 50/50 blend of ads and editorial copy. Using this formula, your cost to print a single page of a program becomes the cost of a half-page advertisement.

Note. All percentages are based on a half-page ad (X).

Size and description	Price as a percentage of X
Full page inside	210
Half page inside	100
Quarter page inside	60
Eighth page inside	40
Sixteenth page inside	25
Back cover (exclusive)	300
Inside front cover	250
Inside back cover	225

Figure 5.14 Advertising costs using Lamonica formula.

afford an ad. While booster ads are not part of Lamonica's formula, you would charge about .15 to .25 of the half-page rate, or $15 to $25.

Small Ads—Large Profits

It should always be more profitable for you to sell many little ads than to sell one big ad on a page. We recommend that you only offer a small number of ad size options, preferably full, half, quarter, eighth, and a patron or booster listing. Working in a number that is easily divisible will also help you lay out ad pages easily. Stay away from thirds of pages—they will drive you crazy, as they do not blend well with half-, quarter-, and eighth-page ads.

The booster listing in this program example, which under the $100 rate established here for a half page would sell for about $25, gives you a chance to mention numerous people on a single page and cover much of the book's cost. A page with two half-page ads pulls in only $200, while a booster club page with 40 listings is worth $1,000. A sample booster page appears in Figure 5.15.

Premium Ad Positions

A premium price should be placed on all cover positions if you wish to sell them. Some people do sell a small streamer ad across the bottom of the front cover. These streamer ads are slightly smaller than a quarter-page vertical ad, but because they appear in the most visible position of the program, they fall into the premium position category. A sample of a program cover including a streamer ad appears in Figure 5.16. The decision to have a streamer ad available on the front cover of your game programs is strictly a matter of personal taste.

Your back cover should sell for three times the half-page rate because it is the most visible ad in the program. The inside front cover should go for 2.5 times the half-page rate, and the inside back cover should go for 2.25 times the half-page rate. If a second, third, or fourth ink color is available for those ads, be sure to add an additional color charge, which can be a flat fee or a percentage. Ask your printer what your cost to run a second color is and figure accordingly, so that you at least recover your costs.

You can also sell center-spread ads at a slightly higher rate. If you change any copy in your program from game to game, the changes should be made on the cover (if it designates the opponent and date of the game) and the center spread section, since it is the most likely location for rosters to appear. Since the roster pages will have the highest visibility other than the cover positions, multiplying the half-page rate by 2.5 will determine the rate, according to the Lamonica formula. For example, if your program includes a scorecard and rosters, a well-placed ad between the two scorecards, or immediately beneath them, is a prime position.

Advertising Selling Schedule

Many sport directors worry about how many times their supporters are hit for money by school teams and other groups. One way to reduce this number is to determine your printing costs for items such as programs, schedule posters, and cards at the beginning of the school year, then sell it as one package.

Ad Copy Collection

When selling ads, stress to the advertiser that the ad should be submitted to you *camera ready*, that is, ready to print in the program. This takes the burden of producing the ad (financial and otherwise) off you and makes your program easier to produce. Give advertisers the exact sizes available and other technical information that your printer can help you with. You may want to print up a sheet with ad rates, sizes, and other specifications, commonly known as a *rate card*. A sample rate card appears in Figure 5.17.

If someone hands you the proverbial table napkin or scrap piece of paper with what they want for an ad on it, inform the party you can have your printer design it and you will only charge your cost. Provide a proof of the ad for the advertiser to approve before going to press, and send a separate bill for the composition of the ad. Design and typesetting of ads can be extra work for you, but it can be a valuable service to your advertisers and good public relations. If you're doing booster or patron ads, the cost of the typesetting is included in the ad.

This is what a full page of booster listings would look like in a souvenir program. You can determine the size of the type and the length of message for each booster.

We Back The Brittons!

Dr. Timothy Williams, DDS
Wilson's Corner Store
Handyman Hardware—2 Locations
Archway Supermarkets
Big Sports Deli
Johnny Gibson's Music Shop
Sheridan Outer Six Theatres
Bethany Hill Church
The Corner Barber Shoppe
Wakefield's Party Store
Mr. & Mrs. Theodore Kallman
State Representative William Charles
Tunes By T—Music & More
Stallworth Studios
Towner's Chicken & Ribs
Quality Bakery
Downtown Health Club
Jen's Dinner Buffet
One Hour Photo Lab of Washington
WJRJ Radio
The Computer Store
Washington Hitching Post
The Reading Rack
Suburban Strip Mall

Figure 5.15 Sample booster listings.

Some may wish to sell advertising on the program cover. A streamer ad placed below the artwork can become a hot item for your advertising sales force to push.

Copper County League

199_ Girls Gymnastics Finals
March 1 • Heritage H.S.

See It Tonight . . . Read About It Tomorrow!
The Best Sports Coverage Is In. . .
THE PIONEER PRESS
Call 555.5555 For Home Delivery

Figure 5.16 Sample program cover with streamer ad.

The rate card provides information essential to those parties you are contacting about advertising. It does not have to be printed on "card" weight paper, but many are. Others, like the sample shown below, serve the dual purpose as a rate card and an advertising order form. This could be printed on carbonless paper or as a single sheet that could be easily photocopied so your client will have a record.

Meridian High School Basketball Program Advertising Rates

Ad type (check desired size)	**Measurements**	**Cost**
☐ Back cover	7 1/2 x 10	$750
☐ Inside front cover	7 1/2 x 10	$600
☐ Inside back cover	7 1/2 x 10	$550
☐ Full page	7 1/2 x 10	$500
☐ Half page	7 1/2 x 4 7/8	$240
☐ Quarter page	3 3/4 x 4 7/8	$150
☐ Eighth page	1 7/8 x 2 7/16	$95
☐ Patron listing		$30

Editions/circulation: 12 home games; 10,000

Space reservations: Space must be reserved at least 6 weeks before first home game

Copy deadline: Copy must be submitted at least 4 weeks before first home game

Special position: Specific ad locations can be guaranteed only for inside front cover, inside back cover, and back cover

Bleeds: No bleeds allowed

Artwork specifications: Use 133- or 150-line screen art for best results; camera-ready ads preferred; advertisers using multiple screens must provide own knockouts; typesetting available at cost; furnished materials returned upon request

For more information contact: Joe Shablotnik, Athletic Director, Meridian H.S., One Hawk Drive, Meridian, 55555; Telephone: 555.555.5555 (Fax: 555.555.5556)

Meridian High School reserves the right to reject or modify an ad deemed to be incompatible with the general tenor and quality of its publication.

Name of advertiser: ______________________

Contact person: ______________________

Address: ______________________

City/State/Zip: ______________________

Voice phone/fax phone: ______________________

Authorized signature/date: ______________________

Ad cost: ______________________

Additional instructions: ______________________

____

Figure 5.17 Sample rate card.

Proof All Ads

Even if you are making everyone submit camera-ready copy for the advertisements in your programs, proof everything you receive before sending it to print. Two examples demonstrate why.

An ad for a summer camp was to promote the fact that it created *winners* out of participants and their families. However, when the camera-ready ad arrived at the printer, it read, "Wining athletes - Wining coaches - Wining parents." After some bad jokes about a little cheese to go with that "whine," the printer set a line of type to cover the error and made the party placing the ad look as good as it thought it would when it submitted the ad.

The other example arose from a state tournament program in which a local sports medicine clinic ran an ad with a staged picture of a team taken during a practice. The only problem was that the players all wore the game uniform of their school, with the school name clearly visible, a violation of that state athletic association's amateur practices rules. Two phone calls later, a substitute ad was made available for the program.

Ads Traded for Products and Services

One other option you can exercise with advertising in your program is to trade advertising space for services rendered. For example, the printer who is producing your program might give you a discount on the job in trade for an advertisement in the book. You could also trade with other businesses in your community for items such as hot dogs for the concession stand or equipment. Just remember that you have to bear the cost of putting the ad in the program, so compare the price of what you're getting to the cost of running the ad.

For example, if your cost to get a page into print is $100, and you want to trade a page of advertising for services or product, attempt to get the rate card value of the page in goods or services. Those businesses have a rate card price, too, and some negotiation will generally be in order. In most cases, you come out paying less through trade than you would in cash, but be careful.

Typesetting

Getting your concepts into print is your responsibility, not your printer's. The old phrase "garbage in, garbage out" certainly applies here. As previously mentioned, give your printer the most complete information for the publication at one time. Avoid providing copy in a piecemeal fashion, and if you must do so, agree to a schedule with your printer for when selected portions of the publication will be submitted.

You have several options available for submitting that copy. The traditional method is putting everything on paper, which is known as *hard copy*.

Hard Copy

Your hard copy should be in a very readable form to expedite the typesetting process. Submit your copy double-spaced to your printer. Avoid submitting single-spaced items, and don't clip something out of another publication and ask your printer to work from it—retype it if you can.

Copy on Computer Disks

With advancements in typesetting methods, you can take copy generated on a word processor, copy that file to a disk, and give it to your printer with a hard copy backup or send it to your printer via modem. Many print shops can now convert word processing files into typeset files, saving much time, and if you typed everything correctly, with fewer errors.

Desktop Publishing

Another option is to do the typesetting in desktop publishing, if available at your school, and submit that disk to your printer. Many printers, however, caution that it sometimes takes longer to rework what a customer has submitted in desktop publishing than to work from a hard copy or text file submitted on a disk.

Another myth about desktop publishing is that you save money in the process, which is only true if you have a person who works with the program every day. Otherwise, you'll spend all your cost savings (and probably more) in the time it takes to prepare it for the printer.

As we discussed previously, some word processing programs are powerful enough for simple desktop publishing tasks, and printing the pages out on a laser printer can be an effective way of producing a finished product.

Proofing

A necessary evil of program production is proofing. It's cumbersome and time consuming, but a necessity. Your most important proofing occurs before you submit your original copy to the printer, and after you receive the first set of proofs that come back for your review.

After returning the first set of proofs for corrections, keep changes to an absolute minimum. The more changes you make, the more the program costs! This is especially true once you reach the final proof, which is referred to as the *blue* or *silver*, named by the color of the image you see. Not only are changes here costly, but they consume time. Make a change any time if you must, but don't be lax with your proofing early, thinking someone else will catch it later. That person may be the parent you hear from the day after the game!

Special Publications

Some schools produce several other publication types on an annual or other scheduled basis for their athletic program, including

- yearbooks and media guides,
- record books, and
- special occasion publications.

We won't discuss specifics about these publications, but you should be aware of these options. Many of the concepts regarding production, costs, and other issues apply to these publications as well.

Some high schools produce yearbooks like college and professional teams. They are generally sport specific and contain in-depth information about that team, its outlook for the coming season, and some other background information about players, coaches, and playing facilities. They may also include all single-game, season, and career statistical records, as well as yearly results for that sport. A separate records book may be produced, but generally not in quantity.

Some schools produce publications to commemorate special occasions, including a major anniversary for that sport at the school, homecoming ceremonies, an anniversary in a major rivalry, or a celebration of a season's achievements.

ALTERNATIVE PRINTED MATERIALS

Print promotions are not limited to ink on paper. You can promote your program and generate funds with souvenir items like buttons and t-shirts. A complete program of this nature could constitute another chapter for this book. Instead, we provide a summary of what buttons and t-shirt promotions can do for your program, including

- building pride in the program in general and a given team specifically, and
- providing another opportunity to promote an event, a team, the school, or an achievement.

Among the most popular buttons are those bearing a picture of a uniformed player, proudly worn by parents. There are also instant cameras available to schools into which a form is inserted with a message or design. When a picture of the subject is shot, the message or design shows up on the photo. A kit is also provided with the camera to cut the photo to fit into a button.

When a team advances to the final round of a state tournament, it's not unusual for someone to print shirts to be worn at the game, or even printed speculatively, to be donned when the championship is won. Schools in medium to large-sized cities have a wide option of vendors to approach regarding the printing of t-shirts and other souvenirs. Sometimes a school may go through the same company from which it orders its game uniforms for t-shirts and sweatshirts.

The typical relationship between a button or shirt vendor and a school is one where the school simply purchases the items from the vendor, and the vendor suggests a recommended resale price for the items. That margin becomes the school's profit on each item.

Purchasing items from a vendor may be done at a discount if enough pieces are ordered. In general, a vendor will give a school a fair discount because of volume and its desire to be involved with your program. Don't expect many donations of product in this area. You might get such items at the vendor's cost, but you'll rarely get it free!

Some schools routinely sell shirts, hats, buttons, mini megaphones, pennants, and many other items at their home games. The trick is to avoid dating anything so that unsold materials from one season can be saved for the next except, of course, when a team is commemorating an outstanding season.

DeWhat?!?

A statewide newspaper includes as part of its high school coverage predictions of tournament games in selected sports. Its famed predictor lightens up the predictions with a play on words using the school or community name.

In this instance, the DeWitt, Michigan High School football team was on a roll in the playoffs in 1989. But when the newspaper predictions came out each week, the writer called the school names from DeWhat to DeWhere. When the team advanced to the state finals at the Pontiac Silverdome, the writer was presented with a shirt from an enterprising party with the inscription

DeWhat?
DeWitt!
DeWhere?
DeDome!

EVALUATING YOUR PRINT PROMOTION EFFORTS

Many of your print promotions cannot be tied to ticket sales, so they are hard to measure. For items such as schedule posters and pocket schedules, monitor your print totals, where they are distributed, and the quantity distributed at each location. Solicit feedback on pocket schedule distribution points to determine levels of interest, assisting you in determining print totals for the following season or year. Advertiser interest will also help determine which projects will continue to be attractive options.

When tracking your game program sales, develop a chart for each sport with headings for date, day of week, opponent, attendance, and programs printed and sold.

This chart will assist you in determining quantities for the following year. It is important to note the day of the week on which the game is played, as mid-week games are generally not as well attended as weekend games. Also make notations about the win-loss record of each team, and whether anything special took place at a game (e.g., homecoming).

Summary

To use print promotions effectively,

1. develop newspaper promotions to help publicize your program's game schedules and other events;
2. produce pocket schedules and schedule posters, selecting from a variety of styles and production options available;
3. develop souvenir game programs;
4. consider special publication projects you might develop locally for a selected event or to celebrate a special occasion;
5. consider alternative printed items, such as buttons and t-shirts, and how they can be integrated into your promotion program; and
6. evaluate your print promotions.

Chapter 6
Promotion Through Mass Media

In this chapter you will learn

1. that a variety of free mass media opportunities can help you promote your program,
2. how to create promotional opportunities on the airwaves to increase public awareness,
3. that putting your games on the radio or local cable is easier than you think, and
4. which opportunities in other communication areas are at your disposal now or will be in the not-too-distant future.

We increasingly rely on electronic devices for information, and radio, television, and the growing information superhighway are available, essential means for promoting your program. Chapter 4 discussed how to accommodate radio and television coming to your events, but this chapter places the shoe on your foot.

COMMON PROMOTION VEHICLES IN MASS MEDIA

Because schools are nonprofit organizations, they qualify for free air time on radio and television stations and on many cable television systems. A variety of avenues are available.

Public Service Announcements and Community Calendars on Radio and TV Stations

Public service announcements (PSAs) are often filler for times when a station hasn't sold any commercials, but they are required by federal law to air so many each day. Even if something you send a station is relegated to the wee hours of the night, you can be certain someone will let you know they heard your announcement.

Some stations take a different approach to PSAs, airing a community calendar, or bulletin board, listing a variety of activities being staged in the area that day or week. Such segments are broadcast at regularly scheduled times throughout the day. Contact a station and ask for the person in charge of PSAs or the community calendar to see what a station's guidelines are for this type of promotion.

You can use either of these opportunities to promote team tryouts and physicals, fund-raising activities, and athletes' achievements. Sometimes promoting a worthwhile cause, such as a student pledge drive for end-of-year activities to be alcohol and drug free, can involve students as announcers. When television stations produce such spots, it's not unusual for participants to wear school uniforms.

Figure 6.1 is a series of sample public service announcements. A good public service announcement is made up of the following elements:

- Who—your school
- What—the event
- When—date and time
- Where—location
- How to get more information (usually a contact name or office and telephone number)
- A *tag* at the end of the announcement which indicates the party responsible for submitting the ad and a place for the station airing the ad to insert its own name
- A time span of 20 to 30 seconds sent to the station at least two weeks in advance of the event

You can type the information on a sheet of paper, or some stations will ask that you put the information on a postcard. When you contact the station, ask which form is preferred.

For television, you may be limited to the community calendar option, and stations will be selective about what they run. Your best chances of getting something on a television station are for fund-raisers, sign up periods for participants, or when physicals are being administered (large- market stations may not use the latter two). You cannot use the community calendar to promote upcoming games; that is what the nightly sportscast does.

You may be able to get some exposure for your program if a local station runs end-of-the-school-year promos to encourage students to avoid drugs and alcohol. Students often appear on camera, sometimes in team uniforms, to help deliver this message.

Cable Television Opportunities

Cable television offers similar opportunities to get your message out. Although not regulated like radio and television, cable systems usually have some kind of channel that carries the messages of non-profit organizations. Some medium to larger systems even dedicate a channel to the local school system.

Contact your local cable system office to obtain the name of the contact person responsible for handling such messages. Some cable outlets provide forms for you to provide information; others work from your scripts.

If you've ever watched these school channels, you know that the lunch menu is often the only information shown. This is a great opportunity to get schedules and other notices out to the community.

Although this channel may be relegated to the higher numbers on your cable box, you might be surprised by how many people see that information. This channel also represents an opportunity to promote your program by showing tapes of games (see pp. 101 and 103 for a detailed discussion of preparing this type of promotion). If you do show games on the channel, write up an announcement with a schedule of what games will be shown along with their playback times. You should also have that information read on the public address system during the actual games.

Other Radio Promotions

Because radio is more affordable than television, you might be able to get one of your advertisers to

(*Note*. Always top each announcement with the following, and send at least 2 weeks in advance of when you want it to begin airing on a station.)

A public service announcement from Your High School
Contact: Joe Dokes, Athletic Director, 555-5555
(Date)
For use between (start date) and (end date)

Physical exams scheduled

Students interested in participating in athletics at Your High School during the 199_–9_ school year are required to undergo physical examinations before they can practice this fall. Physicals will be administered at the school gymnasium on Monday, June 28, and Wednesday, June 30. The cost of the physical is $10. A public service announcement from Your High School and station's call letters or tag.

Soccer teams sponsor car wash

The boys and girls soccer teams of Your High School will be sponsoring a car wash to raise money for new uniforms for the 199_–9_ season. The car wash will take place in the south parking lot at Your High School from 9 a.m. until 2 p.m. on Saturday, August 2. Donations will be accepted for each car washed. Support Panther soccer's work to raise money for new uniforms on August 2. A public service announcement from Your High School and station's call letters or tag.

Booster club outing

The annual Your High School Athletic Booster Club Golf Outing will take place at Mountain Valley Country Club on Friday, July 10, beginning at 9 a.m. Funds raised from this year's outing will go to purchase equipment for the weight room at the high school. For more information, call Your High School Athletic Office at 555-5555 or Mountain Valley Country Club at 777-7777. A public service announcement from Your High School and station's call letters or tag.

Your High School supports good sports

During the 199_–9_ school year, Your High School will join a statewide campaign to promote good sportsmanship, and the Panthers need your help. When you attend a Panther athletic event this year, treat the other team the way you would like to be treated—with respect. A public service announcement from Your High School and station's call letters or tag.

Your High School needs coaches

If you have ever thought of coaching school sports, Your High School athletic department is looking for volunteer assistant coaches for its freshman and junior varsity teams in several sports this year. For more information, contact the school athletic department at 555-5555. A public service announcement from Your High School and station's call letters or tag.

(continued)

Figure 6.1 Sample public service announcements.

AN MHSAA™ PSA

michigan high school athletic association

1019 Trowbridge Road • East Lansing, MI 48823 • 517/332-5046 • FAX 517/332-4071
Contact: John Johnson or Dayna Welch

SUPPORT CAMPAIGN TO ELIMINATE TAUNTING FROM SCHOOL SPORTS

For use between 9/1/94 and 12/3/94

High school sports are different from other levels of athletics because they promote lifelong values—including respect for others. Good Sports Are Winners! because they believe that **Trash Talk is TRASH!** Support the campaign to eliminate taunting from school sports. A public service message from the Michigan High School Athletic Association and (**your station's call letters**).

Figure 6.1 *(continued)*

purchase a radio spot on a local station to promote an upcoming event. The message would end with a tag, acknowledging the business that purchased the ad. This is the broadcast equivalent of the newspaper promotion in which a company paid for a clip and save ad with a team schedule.

You might also be able to get an advertiser to purchase the time to produce a weekly program featuring interviews with coaches. The program would run 3 to 5 minutes, consisting of a program opener, two brief interview segments, and two commercials for the sponsor.

Another twist on the weekly coaches' show is to get several advertisers together to sponsor a weekly coaches corner program. Some stations air programs like this for 30 minutes to an hour, usually live on Saturday mornings. Some coaches talk about their games from the night before, and other coaches talk about their teams. These programs usually originate from the sponsor's place of business, making a restaurant or sporting goods store an ideal sponsor. They usually work very well in communities with more than one high school, providing more variety for listeners.

GAMES ON THE RADIO

In some communities, stations do not broadcast games because they lack the staff. High schools can follow the lead of some colleges and minor league professional teams, securing the air time from a station to broadcast their own originations of a game.

You can either buy the time from the station, or barter the games to them, with the school and the station splitting the available commercial minutes within each broadcast and each party selling its portion. In either case, you would be responsible for costs of getting the games on the air, covering expenses such as equipment, telephone line costs, announcer fees, and travel expenses. If the station isn't interested in doing the games itself, it probably will not be interested in a barter arrangement. You will likely have to buy the air time and sell all the commercial time yourself.

More Student Involvement

The Federal Communications Commission has granted radio broadcasting licenses to some school districts. Having a radio license may supply an opportunity to promote your program by broadcasting athletic events and it gives students broadcasting experience.

Students gain invaluable experience by announcing and producing athletic contests for radio broadcast. Although listening to student radio productions can be trying, involving kids promotes the school's mission.

Start-up costs will be lower if the school district already owns the equipment. The smaller broadcast signal presents challenges because fewer homes receive it compared with a commercially operated station's signal. And sponsors who might provide financial backing are limited to fewer on-air mentions during the game.

But if you have seen the excitement on the faces of young men and women having an opportunity to broadcast the athletic exploits of their peers to their community, you know it's something more schools should try.

Costs

When projecting your costs for a nine-game football schedule with five home games, you know your base costs are going to include installing a telephone line in your press box and keeping it active for at least 3 months (leave the line in long enough for any playoff games that may be played at your field) and installing lines for your away games.

If you find the cost of installing lines for away games prohibitive, consider cellular phones, scanners, transmitters, co-op lines, or doing the away games on a tape-delayed basis. Depending on how far away the game is, you might be able to shuttle the first half tape to the station for playback as soon as that part of the game ends.

You also have to calculate what you will pay announcers, statisticians, and engineers per game, as well as travel costs. If you have to purchase equipment (mixing board, announcer's headsets, telephones, etc.), you will have those one-time costs as well. Here's an example of a budget for a nine-game football season with five home games:

• Mixing board	$350
• Microphones and headsets	$500
• Tape recorder	$75
• Telephone and coupler (actual instrument)	$100
• Telephone line installation (5 sites)	$750*
• Long-distance charges (4 games)	$150
• Announcer fees (2 at $50 per game)	$900
• Travel expenses	$200
• Miscellaneous	$100
Total	**$3,125**

*This figure could be cut at least in half if your opponents all originate games and install co-op lines for visiting stations to use.

Selling Your Game Package

Once you have assembled your game package, you have to sell it. Again, you need a lot of advance planning, but you could set up a package for your local advertisers to purchase program, schedule card, and radio broadcast advertising simultaneously. Potential advertisers would rather be approached for a combined package than hit at separate times for separate buys.

Base your charges on your costs and game format. The format (see Figure 6.2) is what you use to determine commercial placement and the order of topics to discuss between plays.

Format

During a 2-hour radio broadcast, it wouldn't be unusual to have 20 minutes of commercial time available. If broadcasting nine games with a projected cost of $400 per game, your spot rate would need to be around $10 per 30-second commercial just to break even. You would then have to find perhaps five sponsors at $80 per game. Another option would be to charge $150 per game per sponsor with a goal of five sponsors, but hitting the break-even point

Your High School
Basketball Radio Format

(On air at 7:20 p.m.)

Taped program open w/billboards

Opening comments from play-by-play

Break #1 — 2:00

Al's Restaurant	:30
Dairy King	:30
Milk Producers	:30
Diet Soda	:30

Taped interview with Coach Brown

Break #2 — :60

Marshall Ford	:30
Your Town Parks and Rec	:30

Starting lineups and analysis

Break #3 — 2:00

Al's Restaurant	:30
Dairy King	:30
Milk Producers	:30
Diet Soda	:30

First quarter

Timeout called

Break #4 — :60

Marshall Ford	:30
Your Town Parks and Rec	:30

End of first quarter

Break #5 — :60

Pace Hardware	:30
Meridian Mall	:30

Second quarter

Timeout called

Break #6 — :60

Al's Restaurant	:30
Dairy King	:30

End of first half

Break #7 — 2:00

Milk Producers	:30
Diet Soda	:30
Marshall Ford	:30
Your Town Parks and Rec	:30

First half review — promo halftime interview

Break #8 — 2:00

Pace Hardware	:30
Meridian Mall	:30
Milk Producers	:30
Diet Soda	:30

Halftime interview with Joe Dokes, cross country coach

Break #9 — 2:00

Milk Producers	:30
Diet Soda	:30
Marshall Ford	:30
Your Town Parks and Rec	:30

Review of first half scoring and statistics

Break #10 — 2:00

Pace Hardware	:30
Meridian Mall	:30
Milk Producers	:30
Diet Soda	:30

Third quarter

Timeout called

Break #11 — :60

Marshall Ford	:30
Your Town Parks and Rec	:30

End of third quarter

Break #12 — :60

Pace Hardware	:30
Meridian Mall	:30

Fourth quarter

Timeout called

Break #13 — :60

Al's Restaurant	:30
Dairy King	:30

End of game

Break #14 — 2:00

Milk Producers	:30
Diet Soda	:30
Marshall Ford	:30
Your Town Parks and Rec	:30

Game review

Break #15 — 2:00

Pace Hardware	:30
Meridian Mall	:30
Milk Producers	:30
Diet Soda	:30

Postgame interview with assistant coach or head coach

Break #16 — 2:00

Milk Producers	:30
Diet Soda	:30
Marshall Ford	:30
Your Town Parks and Rec	:30

Review of stats — closing comments

Taped program close w/billboards

Figure 6.2 Sample radio format.

with the third. Packaged with some of the items listed previously, you might be able to incorporate radio as part of a comprehensive sponsorship program that not only covers costs of several projects, but raises additional monies for the athletic program.

When approaching sponsors for the radio broadcasts, your approach should be that you are providing a community service by airing games for those people who cannot attend in person and that a company's support will also help support that program financially. A sample letter appears in Figure 6.3.

When formatting a game, make it sound as professional as possible, with planned segments during pregame, postgame, and halftime. If coaches are agreeable, you might include a taped interview during the pregame segment. You might also talk with a player. Avoid the most common high school broadcast mistake: filling the 5 to 10 minutes of pregame with idle chatter and commercials.

Halftime can be a marvelous vehicle to sell your school and programs other than major athletic teams. (No disrespect to marching bands, but unless you have the appropriate microphones on the field, you really cannot present a representative halftime show of just music.) Arranging to have a live or taped interview with the coach of a low-profile sport, or from a school club, can help promote the total school program. You could also present a schedule of upcoming school events for that week. The possibilities are limited only by your imagination and work ethic.

This idea still works if the local station originates your games. Technically, the games are the property of the school, not the radio station. However, you should approach broadcasters with a spirit of partnership. Offer to help the station by providing or performing pregame or halftime interviews, or providing short notes about school events or groups that could be read on the air. This approach improves your chances for broadcasting to become a communications vehicle for your school.

ANNOUNCERS

If you find yourself in a position to select the announcers for these broadcasts, ensure that that individual is competent in play-by-play or analysis, understands what high school sports are all about, and has enough personality to make the games sound exciting without being too biased. Again, you can have total control when you package the games yourself. Often, you have little input, if any, when the station originates the games.

TELEVISION PROMOTIONS

On-air television promotions operate in a manner similar to radio promotions, but television promotions are much more expensive and are generally cost prohibitive for school program involvement.

Cable television, however, is a different matter. Depending on the capabilities of your local system, you may be able to produce games and other programs yourself (if the local cable company is not already doing so). If airing videotapes is not an option, see if you can provide the cable company with an audio feed for a radio-style broadcast of your games. Sometimes radio stations that are only allowed to broadcast during daylight hours make arrangements with the local cable company to air their audio on a channel dedicated to showing messages.

Multi-Camera Productions

Some schools have television facilities with remote equipment that allows them to produce multiple-camera originations of contests (generally home games) to be shown on a designated channel on a tape-delayed basis. If this equipment is available to you, you may wish to assemble a volunteer crew to produce a number of games during the year. You may be able to solicit some support for your minimal hard costs (such as videotape stock), acknowledging those businesses during the game. Commercials are not likely to appear on a school-produced origination. Many of the same formatting principles discussed in originating your own radio broadcasts also apply here. However, when broadcasting a game on tape delay, you have the ability to stop the tape during breaks in the action, including halftime.

Tailor this letter to use as a potential first contact with a prospective advertiser. In this case, the letter is selling the radio package, but a letter could also be used to sell print advertising or general sponsorships.

Dobie High School Athletics

Home of the Fighting Rams

1234 Dobie Road • Dobie, XX 98765

555.555.5555 (FAX - 555.555.5556)

June 6, 199_

Ms. Jane Milan
Owner
The Runner's Edge
Dobie Mall
Dobie, XX 98765

Dear Ms. Milan:

Welcome to the exciting world of interscholastic athletics. Dobie High School promotes an educationally sound athletic program for student-athletes in which we seek to make a young man's or woman's experience meaningful. We hope to provide students with memories that will last a lifetime.

Creating those memories means recognizing these young people for being involved in our events. It also means servicing the community in which we live in a way that everyone can be involved. We need your help to make these dreams happen for these young people and our town.

This year Dobie High School will broadcast all of its home and away contests in football and in boys and girls basketball. Please take a few moments to review the enclosed materials, detailing our advertising packages for the upcoming school year. We hope you will find these proposals attractive—not only from an advertising perspective, but from the position that you will be engaging in a positive public relations endeavor that should pay future dividends for your company. The enclosed rate card and contract detail the program in its entirety.

I will contact you in a few days to discuss this matter further. If you have any questions, feel free to contact me at 555.5555.

Thank you for your consideration. I look forward to speaking with you soon.

Cordially,

Joan Robinson
Athletic Director

JR/ibm

Enclosures

Figure 6.3 Sample letter to advertisers.

Single-Camera Productions

Another video promotion option is to take game footage shot with a single camera and play it back on an available channel on the cable system. This video could be shot by a spectator, be the coach's game video, or be shot by a dedicated camera from the same vantage point as the coach's video. The main difference between the coach's video and the dedicated camera video is that the coach's video is generally shot with a very wide view of the field.

An important caution about single-camera productions is that you should have a good idea of how the tape looks and sounds before airing it. Some editing may be necessary. You might be able to hook a microphone into the camera to provide play-by-play commentary, or with the permission of your local radio station, you may be able to use the radio station's description of the game on your tape. If your team is participating in its state tournament, check with your state athletic association before airing any tapes to see if any regulations apply to the playback of game tapes on cable or on-air television.

Videotape Promotions

Videotapes commemorating a season are not uncommon at the professional and college levels. On occasion, some high schools have produced highlights tapes as fund-raisers. These tapes include a variety of footage, including regular-season and tournament footage, pep assemblies, and shots of the team boarding the bus and rolling through the decorated downtown streets of an excited community.

Editing equipment available to individuals and schools allows for some special effects to be added to such productions, providing fans with a bona fide keepsake of a season. Usually the person editing the tape is producing it out of deep affection for the team and may ask to be reimbursed only for hard costs (but often they don't ask at all).

Again, check with your state high school athletic association regarding the use of tournament footage in such tapes. In general, the state athletic association owns the video rights to its tournament games, regardless of who shoots the video.

Student Involvement

Strive to involve students in radio and television promotions. Some professional broadcasters got their starts as spotters, statisticians, or announcers on local radio, television, or cable originations of high school games. Serving as a camera operator, director, or in any other technical function is also appealing to students.

Technology is constantly changing, and it sounds trite, but only your imagination will limit you here. Watch for these avenues to be utilized in the future.

- Computer bulletin boards. Local versions of some of the popular online computer services already provide information about school athletic events.
- The Internet. Having information about your teams available on the Internet to callers from all points (remember that your alumni spread out around the country) is now a reality at the college and professional levels of sports.
- Fax-on-demand. A dedicated computer connected to a telephone line (like a bulletin board) can be used to distribute information via fax. There are two types of fax-on-demand services: the one-call service, in which individuals wanting information call fax-on-demand from their fax machines, or the two-call method, in which callers dial fax-on-demand from any touch-tone telephone, then input the telephone number of the fax machine to receive the information. In both instances, the party responsible for making the information available faxes it first to the fax-on-demand service. Callers input access codes from their touch-tone telephones to request certain documents.
- Telephone services. Like a computer bulletin board or fax-on-demand service, a phone

line can be connected to a computer to provide team schedules and other information. A variety of mailboxes store different messages, and a caller can access the information by hitting a series of buttons on a touch-tone telephone. Some services also allow you to make the radio broadcasts of your games available to people who call in and listen after charging the call to a credit card.

For any of these services, you can sell advertising opportunities to help defray your expenses.

EVALUATING YOUR MASS MEDIA EFFORTS

Like any other portion of your promotions program, evaluation is needed to keep track of the progress you make in this area. Every promotion needs to be inventoried and accounted for to assist you in the decision-making process for future years.

A mass media plan is difficult to tie to attendance. Keep track of the public service announcements you provide to stations, and ask for proof of those messages airing. Proof of performance by stations tells you how many times your PSAs were aired and the time of day they were broadcast. Remember, in some communities, your school is not the only party seeking air time through PSAs. While a station is obligated to run PSAs, it does reserve the right to decide which ones they will use and how many times they will air.

Anything for which you sell advertising can be gauged as a success as long as businesses are willing to provide support. Many mass media opportunities depend upon a mix of dollars and exposure to determine their success. You will find that if you can get your costs underwritten and the community is pleased, then that project is worth continuing. There are some projects (like radio and television broadcasts) which could be financially profitable for your school as well.

As far as originating your games is concerned, listen for community comments. You will not be able to measure anything here.

Some of the new technology options may be able to track how many callers use the services and which services they use most.

Summary

To promote your program through the mass media,

1. understand that radio, on-air, and cable television offer some common promotional avenues,
2. use radio opportunities for exposure beyond commercial and public service announcements,
3. obtain exposure by originating games on radio and cable television,
4. raise funds through the sale of videotapes commemorating outstanding seasons, and
5. use the information superhighway to promote prep sports.

Chapter 7

Developing Special Promotions

Many school people reminisce about the so-called *good old days* when the stands were packed at high school games every Friday night. The only problem about those days was that football and boys basketball were nearly the only games in town, and those who didn't actually participate in the games were in the stands. The only opportunity available to girls was to cheer.

Today's kids enjoy many more opportunities, and the spectator base hasn't changed; people just attend different events. Athletics also face competition from cable television and malls, and more high school students than ever before hold jobs after school. These changes dictate that we do the best job possible to promote our product.

A fan attending a high school state championship event recently paid $4.00 to watch four games, then talked on and on about how enjoyable the day was, what a great deal it was for family entertainment, and how the kids exclaimed on the way home "Let's go back again!" In these days of triple-figure ticket costs for professional athletic events and concerts, and when a family of four can't attend a major college football game for less than $100, the high school ticket becomes easy to promote.

But you have to think like a promoter to be successful. Wins bring out fans in droves in communities in which the high school team is the only game in town. In highly populated areas where the options on game nights abound, you have to get creative. In earlier chapters, we explored a variety of methods for promoting your sport program, but their direct effects on attendance are almost impossible to measure. As we look at developing special promotions, we enter an area in which success is determined by the number of people in the stands.

This chapter examines

1. how every ticket sold, even at a discount, represents additional revenue opportunities once the spectator arrives at an event;
2. how to conduct a variety of promotions connected with an actual game to boost attendance; and
3. how in-game promotions and giveaways promote an atmosphere that draws people back again and again.

TICKETS

Professional athletic venture promoters who have numerous dates to sell tickets for learned long ago to develop a different promotion for each game. Some say this practice reduces full-price ticket sales, but given the choice between filling half the house with full-price tickets or filling it with a promotion, the full house is a better option.

More Revenue Opportunities With More Tickets Sold

A full house provides numerous money-making opportunities, including concessions, souvenirs, drawings, parking, and programs. The list goes on and on. A fan brought in on a promotion might only return on other special nights, but they may also come back as full-price patrons. Cultivate your crowd for the future by looking beyond the single-game, full-price ticket.

The Season Ticket

The season ticket is immensely popular at schools with long traditions of winning in a particular sport. Some of these schools even sell a reserved seat ticket. Testimony to the season ticket appears in schools with strong basketball traditions in Indiana, where a waiting list for season tickets has existed at some schools for years, and season tickets are literally handed down in wills when people die. This example is extreme, but suggests what can happen.

Hoosier Hysteria

A former Indiana sports writer reported that before constructing a new gymnasium, Warsaw High School sold nearly every one of its 3,000 seats on a season-ticket basis for boys basketball games. Visiting schools were often limited to less than 100 tickets when playing there.

In the book, *Hoosiers (The Fabulous Basketball Life of Indiana)*, author Philip House tells how 17 families in Anderson have held season tickets to Anderson High School boys basketball games since the Great Depression. In that city of over 65,000 residents, the three high schools sell over 15,000 season tickets. When changes in the automotive industry gave Anderson the nation's highest unemployment rate in the 1980s, people still found the means to hold onto their season tickets to their favorite school.

Even if demand is high, good promoters sell season tickets for convenience and because spectators desire discounts, however small they may be. Promoters commonly discount the season ticket by the cost of one or two single-game tickets. For example, if your football team plays five home games and a single-game adult ticket costs $5, you might sell the public season ticket at $15 to $20, possibly less, and price student season tickets similarly.

Season Ticket Variations

Also consider a family season ticket, providing a slightly greater discount over the standard season ticket. For example, if the adult season ticket for the aforementioned football season was $20, and the student season ticket for the same was $10, a family of four season ticket might cost $50 or less instead of $60.

You might also sell a partial season ticket. For example, this ticket could include just half the number of home games, or selected home games, with a slight discount. Another variation is a four-by-four concept, under which someone buys four tickets for four games. You can adjust any of these options to meet your needs.

The All-Year Ticket

An extension of the season ticket, the all-year ticket is sold as a fund-raiser at the beginning of the year, providing the bearer admission to all events during the season. This a great way to attract fans to events they might not typically attend and can be offered at student, public, and family rates.

Determine the price of this ticket by dividing the number of home events you're planning for a given year by two to four, then multiplying by the average cost of a full-price ticket. Ensure that this ticket costs less than it would to purchase season tickets for football, boys basketball, and girls basketball (generally the most popular sports) combined. Some schools sell such tickets to adults for about $40 each. Most purchasers won't attend all events, so you're likely to generate new revenues.

Limits

To avoid overselling tickets, set limits based on the history of attendance at your events and your seating capacity. Also remind people that if all special tickets are general admission, seating is on a space-available basis. But to maintain good public relations, avoid overselling the house!

GAME SPECIALS

You can run a variety of specials for individual games, picking one special for selected home games (not necessarily all home games—you're hoping that those who come in on discounted tickets earlier in the season will return later at full price). Game specials involve offering discounts to selected groups for a particular night. A few examples follow.

Family Discounts

A great family discount package provides a family of four that purchases tickets for a game with food from the concession stand. Using the *four for four* concept, a family of four receives tickets, four soft drinks, four hot dogs, and four bags of popcorn at a discounted price. Again, you come out ahead because that family might never purchase all these food items at regular price, and items like pop and popcorn are almost all profit to begin with.

Senior Citizens

Senior citizens can be another target group, especially if you can generate goodwill between the school and a retirement community by having students bring retirees to a game at no charge. Many business establishments offer discounts to senior citizens; you can do the same.

Theme and Other Special Nights

Your variety of discount promotions is limited only by your imagination and the makeup of your community. Themes could include two for one, parent/child nights (father/daughter or mother/son), alumni, school colors, posters, churches (for private schools, offering a discount for bringing a church bulletin from the previous Sunday), union workers, service organizations, honor roll students, and local youth recreation leagues (for kids wearing game jerseys).

Giveaways

Also consider ticket giveaways. You can promote an upcoming game on a local radio station by allowing the station to give away a limited number of tickets. Stations welcome prizes to give away, and you get free air time every time the station mentions the giveaway.

OTHER WAYS TO FILL THE STANDS

Special ticket packages and single-game discounted admissions are not the only ways to get more people interested in attending games, but they can be the centerpiece of many promotions. Numerous opportunities exist to involve different community groups tying their projects to one of your events. You can also stage some of your own attractions.

Community Group Involvement

Becoming involved with community service groups like the Lions, Kiwanis, Elks, Moose, and others, you could set up a promotion to benefit both you and the service organization. One option is to sell tickets to the service organization at a discounted (probably half) price, then have the service organization resell the tickets at face value. You could also allow a service group to stage a drawing for a giveaway item or a contest involving students in an activity like shooting free throws to raise money for that group. These efforts foster a spirit of community and likely bring people who have been away for a long time back to the stands.

Food Promotions

Nothing attracts people like food. Attach a food promotion to a game—like a fish fry, spaghetti dinner, pancakes and sausage, corn roast, or a food court with several options— as a separate attraction or in combination with the cost of a game ticket. These events benefit club or service organizations and promote additional attendance.

Entertainment Promotions

Numerous attractions present options for pregame, halftime, or postgame festivities. A local dance company could perform a 5-minute routine, and Frisbee catching dogs have been popular for a long time. Some of these groups may be contacted through a local college, and unless they're very much in demand, they may perform at little or no cost to you.

Displaying some of your school's talents during your athletic events improves internal public relations and promotes your school's total program to the public. Pom-pom, forensic, dance, and drama groups can put on brief programs. Bands and singing groups could also be involved.

Don't overlook the athletic teams in your elementary school system or your building. You might include a halftime exhibition to support those groups. Remember that coming in with all these performers will be parents and families, who otherwise may not attend until their youngsters reach high school age.

Dances after games, properly supervised, can also be a method of bringing students to contests. To avoid the conflicts that can occur with individuals who engage in undesirable behavior (like drinking) before coming to the dance, you may wish to restrict admission to those who purchase a game admission before halftime of the varsity contest.

In-School Promotions

Students are probably the most important group that you must attract to contests. Their support of fellow students at any school event is vital. Incentives for the class with the best attendance range from free tickets to a pizza party. If you present a prize like a pizza party, see if a local business will underwrite the cost of the product for promotional consideration. You can acknowledge the donation of the product in your game program, in flyers around school before the event, and in public address announcements during the school day and at the game.

You can also conduct poster and cheer contests by class at events. Each class could create a set of posters promoting school spirit to be displayed at a given game, with selected faculty members responsible for judging. The same treatment would work for cheer blocks at a contest. School administration should ensure everything is done in good taste, and local businesses could provide prizes to the winning group.

Fund-Raising Promotions

A well-staged fund-raising promotion, such as giving away a bicycle or something even more valuable, if it requires individuals to be present to win, can be effective. Businesses providing the prize receive much exposure if the promotion is conducted over several weeks, and it provides a point of focus for the event.

Fifty-fifty giveaways, for which tickets are sold for a drawing that provides half the money to your program and the other half to the winning ticket bearer, have been used for a long time, but be careful. A lottery giveaway that promotes a get-rich-quick- or getting-something-without-working-for-it-idea may be incompatible with your mission of educational athletics. If you are hosting a postseason tournament game, check with your state athletic association to see if local promotions of *any* type may be conducted.

League-Wide Promotions

Your school may benefit from collaborating with other schools to promote attendance. One approach involves a special meeting of the sport directors from each school to map out a plan so that each school selects a game at which to stage a promotion to increase attendance. Another variation is to conduct the promotion on a common set of nights so that all schools host the promotion once. Working together, you pool creative talents and gain the ability to market your promotion package to sponsors at one time if potential sponsors serve all affected communities in your conference.

A good idea for a conference promotion is to bestow an award on the school that creates the best game atmosphere, sportsmanship promotion, or gym-filling promotion. The state of Illinois has had great success with its annual Pack the Place promotion.

We Want You To Pack the Place

The Illinois High School Association (IHSA) launched its Pack the Place promotion during the 1987–88 school year and has conducted it annually since. Concerned about the statewide drop in attendance at high school athletic events, particularly among young families without high school aged children, the IHSA board adopted Pack the Place as its first promotion ever.

The promotion challenged schools to select one night during the basketball season to attempt to sell out the gymnasium. Schools reaching 80 percent of their capacity were presented with a commemorative banner to hang in the gym. In 1993–94, 112 schools were honored.

Creative juices soon flowed at IHSA member schools. Discounted tickets, terrible towels, custodians in tuxedos, scorekeepers in sombreros, halftime shoot-outs, and pancake suppers were just a few of the promotions staged. The effort also turned the most skeptical of sports writers into supporters, with editorials appearing in local papers that encouraged fans to participate in the program.

CROSS PROMOTIONS—*The Big Event*

Any idea in this chapter could be combined with another or expanded, involving more than just traditional sports. If you have the physical plant to do so, consider staging a *Big Event*, bringing several varsity teams to play together on one night in conjunction with other activities.

Consider this agenda for a *Big Event*:

- **3:30 p.m.**—Swimming dual meet
- **5:00 p.m.**—Boys/girls varsity basketball game (special pregame/halftime show—school ROTC drill team)
- **6:00 p.m.**—Food court opens
- **6:45 p.m.**—Entertainment by jazz vocal group
- **7:15 p.m.**—Boys/girls varsity basketball game (special halftime show—gymnastics or elementary school basketball/soccer exhibition)
- **8:45 p.m.**—Varsity wrestling match
- **10:00 p.m.**—Pizza party and dance

This schedule brings many people not affiliated with your sport program, even as spectators, into the building paying admission. However, the event may strain your event management staff to supervise or convert facilities from one event to another quickly, or attendance may exceed your capacity. When planning a *Big Event*, closely monitor your personnel and facility capabilities and limitations.

BUSINESS BARTER

When a local business provides a product or service, ensure that they receive appropriate recognition, known as a trade or barter agreement. Appropriate trades include advertising or appearance in the souvenir game program, a public address announcement or sign at the event, and mention as a participating sponsor in promotional materials. Make every effort to recognize that sponsor, and communicate exactly what has been donated to the school.

PROMOTION OF PROMOTIONS

Use the methods described in chapter 4 to publicize your ticket promotions. Getting local businesses to underwrite advertisements in your local newspaper promoting games and special nights promotes community involvement. In fact, if you give them credit as a sponsor, the newspaper may donate advertising space as its contribution to the event.

Also encourage the sponsor to take responsibility for promoting the event. For example, if a local fast food chain helps sponsor an event, that sponsor might promote it with flyers or posters in its stores.

Press releases, in-school public address announcements, and letters to students, parents, and the general public are other ways of getting your message out. If people see the work you're committing, their curiosity may turn them into spectators for future events.

IN-GAME PROMOTIONS

Now that you've developed some strategies for attracting people to your events, you may wish to stage a series of in-game promotions to further enhance your total product and promote school spirit. These promotions fall into three areas: general giveaways, involving a series of giveaway nights; specific giveaways, in which the same promotion runs during every contest; and intermission attractions, in which a contest winner receives a prize.

General Giveaways

The advance planning that goes into general giveaways involves identifying a series of inexpensive products that can be given away at specific games. Such items include, but are not limited to, miniature balls, pom-poms, bells, hats, horns, hankies, towels, and sunglasses.

These giveaways tie in directly with ticket promotions. Generally, promote them in advance, and provide a souvenir item to a set number of spectators, usually based on who comes through the gates first. However, you may occasionally wish to conduct the giveaway as a surprise. Miniature balls thrown into the stands by cheerleaders during the closing moments of a game is a popular practice that keeps spectators guessing about what may happen during an upcoming game.

The key is planning for giveaway items that work in your venue, estimating the costs for those items, then pitching local businesses to purchase them for you in return for their name appearing somewhere on the product and some additional promotion, such as public address announcements. High schools rarely purchase these giveaway items themselves.

Schedule giveaway nights carefully. A giveaway night for every contest will lose appeal and limit your creativity over time. It will also wear out your sponsors.

A Real Bell Ringer

A college had a bell night for one of its ice hockey games. The athletic department split the cost of about 1,500 cow bells with a local fast food restaurant, and the restaurant put a sticker on each bell displaying the slogan "Go Broncos," as well as its logo.

The idea worked great for the fans. It helped ignite the crowd in an important league game, but the bells, especially when they clanged against the aluminum bleacher seats, also made an incredible amount of noise.

Specific Giveaways

Using a set number of specific giveaways has long been popular at all levels of professional sports and even at the college level. An organization gives a sponsor involvement on a game-by-game basis. At the high school level these promotions will likely work best only at sports attracting highest attendance.

Marked Programs

A specific promotion that helps bolster your souvenir program sales involves marking a sponsor's ad with a stamp or serial number. At a predetermined point during the game (usually a break between quarters), the public address announcer reads the number or directs spectators to look in their programs for the marked ad, then instructs the holder of the winning program to report to a designated location to claim a prize from that sponsor.

At the high school level, a stamp is easier to manage than serial numbers (which are generally imprinted at the printer and are more expensive). You could use two or three different stamps, then draw for which is to be used to designate the winning program that day, maintaining an element of suspense before the drawing and keeping security higher.

You can also use game ticket stubs for giveaways. Obtain tickets numbered at both ends so that patrons always receive numbered stubs, retaining them to present following the drawings.

Establish a predetermined number of drawings for each game, using sponsor-provided prizes (one or two per game). Prizes might include a school t-shirt or sweatshirt, coupons for a free pizza or sandwich at a local restaurant, or a free oil change at a local automotive shop.

Seat Location Drawings

Seat locations may also be used for giveaways, but they work best when your seats are theater style or numbered. Another method of giving away prizes involves sticking a token under a specific seat, then having the public address announcer ask everyone to look under their seats for it. If your seats are numbered or reserved, you might announce the section number, row, and seat of the prize recipient. That way, ushers can police those who may try to muscle someone out of a seat or move into an announced seat if vacant when the announcement is made.

The drawback of this method is that if done too often, unscrupulous individuals arriving early may try to scout around for the location of these indicators. Another negative is the additional work that goes into marking seats—picking a ticket out of a hat or reading a number in a program is easier.

CARNIVAL EVENTS

Many of use have seen the individual who makes the halfcourt shot at a basketball game and wins a car. On a smaller scale, these promotions are available to high schools willing to get a local business either to provide the prize in return for a certain amount of recognition or to purchase insurance at a cost below the cost of the prize if it needs to be given away. Some companies specialize in such promotions, selling insurance to schools, betting the prize will not be won.

Score-O in hockey, the halfcourt shot, and anything else your imagination comes up with can be used at different events. Recognize the sponsor of the prize in flyers, your program, and public address announcements. You could also display the prize at the event to provide exposure for the sponsor. You sell the sponsor on the combination of the exposure and the generally low risk of someone actually winning the prize.

TIME MANAGEMENT FOR PROMOTION PLANNING

Form 3.2 (see p. 27) helped you plan the involvement of others in your promotion program. Identifying those individuals to whom you can delegate necessary aspects of promotions (e.g., honor students, volunteer faculty members, or a booster club) is a key to staging successfully anything beyond ticket promotions. Careful planning, communication, and organization enable you and your staff to execute special promotions effectively.

EVALUATING YOUR SPECIAL PROMOTIONS EFFORTS

The same evaluation form used in chapter 3 (see Form 3.3, p. 30) can help you to evaluate your ticket and special promotions. Maintaining records of roles and responsibilities, what sponsors provided, attendance levels, and return received by those involved will assist you in your evaluation. The paper trail will help you steer away from promotions that do not return the results you desire.

Summary

To develop effective special promotions,

1. review the factors mandating that your school sport program enter the promotion arena to attract spectators to events;
2. recognize that ticket promotions provide revenue opportunities for the organization, even for tickets sold at a discount;
3. pursue different promotions, involving community groups or selling food, to attract a different crowd of people to your events whom you can attempt to bring to subsequent contests without promotions;
4. display the talents of other community and in-school groups to showcase their talents and get new spectators in the door;
5. promote a variety of school teams and groups on a single night to create a *Big Event*;
6. involve businesses in trading or bartering services or products for positive promotion;
7. use giveaway items and carnival events at games to promote school spirit, attract spectators, and further involve the community; and
8. document ticket and other special promotions to determine whether they impacted attendance.

Chapter 8 Obtaining Sponsorships

Planning an effective campaign to promote your interscholastic sport program is a year-round effort to unify the school and community. Likewise, your efforts to obtain sponsorships need to point toward year-round involvement.

School districts across the country continually rely on external funding to help make ends meet. To that end, they are looking at programs to minimize the number of times they ask community businesses to get involved and maximize the revenue potential from each source.

So with different degrees of intensity, schools and individual sports teams are entering into the world of corporate sponsorships. The terms *corporate sponsor* or *corporate partner* are not reserved for large events like the World Cup, Olympics, or national collegiate championships. You can craft your own corporate support packages. These packages need not be monetary in nature. In some cases you will need a business to put up some money to underwrite a particular promotion. In other instances you may wish to get the business to donate products or services as its corporate contribution.

Your sponsorship program will differ greatly from packages sold by professional or college teams. Higher levels of athletics depend on sponsorships for daily revenues, but your sponsorships make possible the add-ons to your program, with some potential for additional revenue. Your philosophy will set limits on the amount of commercial involvement in your program. To be successful at obtaining sponsorships, balance what you need and want to protect with the needs of potential sponsors.

In this chapter you will learn

1. how to understand the needs of your potential sponsors,
2. how to identify the elements of your program that may require sponsorship,
3. how to identify potential sponsors and their contributions,
4. how to prepare a sponsorship proposal,
5. how to contact potential sponsors, and
6. how to evaluate your sponsorship program.

UNDERSTANDING A SPONSOR'S NEEDS

Every sponsor, from an international company to the corner convenience store, enters a sponsorship arrangement with certain objectives. As you venture into the business world, working agreements are likely to be more detailed than within your organization, and each sponsor has its own set of expectations. Those expectations range from sponsors happy to be involved because the owner is an alumnus of the school or for potential public relations benefits, to those who may actually look at the *cost per impression* (also known as cost per thousand, meaning the cost to the company for every thousand people who see the message) of a sponsorship.

High schools experience more difficulty delivering an efficient cost per impression than do other sport properties, largely because those sponsorship opportunities are of a larger scope than a local high school program. Give these sponsors the best program you can, but avoid pretending that they are necessarily getting into cost-effective promotions.

A sponsor wants answers to the following questions:

- Does sponsoring the school program or event fit the company's position in the community and nation?
- Is the sponsorship product exclusive (i.e., no other sponsors with a similar product or service will be involved)?
- Can the sponsor be included in the title of the event?
- How much visibility will the sponsor receive from materials like signage and program advertising space?
- What other ways will the sponsor be recognized?
- How many participants and spectators will be exposed to the sponsorship?
- Is there a way for the sponsor to build sales as a result of the sponsorship?
- How much will the sponsorship cost? Can product and services be included?

A sponsor will look to gain the most exposure possible from the least financial investment. Many larger companies happily provide products and services to keep funds in the advertising or sponsorship budget; corporate offices are more flexible about distributing product than spending dollars.

Unless you approach an executive with close ties to your programs, and the company is willing to spend public relations dollars in the community in which it is located, you will run into a bottom-line oriented mind-set when approaching a large company. Smaller business operators may not ask as many questions about the sponsorship. They are often tightly linked to the community, possibly as lifelong residents, and they are usually willing to give back to a system from which they have benefited.

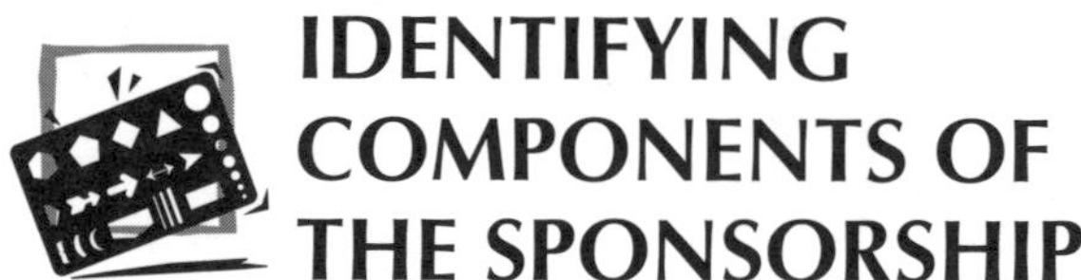

IDENTIFYING COMPONENTS OF THE SPONSORSHIP

A detailed list of sponsorship opportunities includes

- equipment needs (uniforms);
- facility needs (scoreboards, message centers, playing fields);
- advertising support (schedules, programs);
- invitational tournaments (expenses, trophies);
- fund-raising needs (costs of a fund-raising campaign);
- promotional needs (giveaways, carnival event underwriting); and
- awards needs (banquets).

No one entity is likely to cover any single item on your wish list. However, you will generally know whether the potential for a large gift exists at a given time. In general, a high school sport program depends on numerous sponsors. Depending on philosophy, a college, professional team, or sports governing or service agency may opt to have only a handful of large sponsors. Your proposal to a potential sponsor could specify a specific element from those listed previously or include aspects of several. A key is giving a sponsor a range of options.

IDENTIFYING POTENTIAL SPONSORS

Any business in the community is a potential sponsor, and if your school has a history of soliciting funds, you may have a ready-made list to begin working from. If starting from scratch, consult a telephone directory or business directory published by your local Chamber of Commerce. Also keep track of who advertises in your local media on a regular basis. Tracking newspaper, radio, television, and magazine ads gives you a feel for who may have dollars to spend.

Other ideas to develop your potential sponsor list include

1. parents in your program who occupy positions of authority within companies in your town, even if they don't do a lot of local advertising. Sometimes, these companies have money to invest in community projects like yours;
2. watching to see what companies sponsor sporting events in your community specifically, and on a regional, statewide, or national basis in general;
3. looking for businesses new to the area, those looking to promote themselves within the community; and
4. looking for businesses that benefit the most from the presence of your school and its athletic programs. This would include vendors from whom your organization purchases products, or businesses like convenience stores, restaurants, and others located near your school that are frequented by students and faculty daily, and by the community when there is a home event on your campus.

Keep track of your potential sponsors, background information on each, and their history of involvement with you on a computer program. Some of the simple database or even more advanced word processing programs can be used to develop tracking forms. Form 8.1 is a sample sponsorship tracking form (see pp. 120–122).

Once you have assembled your list of potential sponsors, note your feelings for their possible involvement. The local ice cream stand might not be good for more than a patron's listing in your programs or sponsorship of a schedule card for a single-sport season. The fast food restaurant that is part of a chain of 50 stores in your part of the state, run by a local businessman or a soft-drink bottler, might just want to sponsor a tournament or go together to purchase a new scoreboard for your outdoor sports complex.

DEVELOPING THE PROPOSAL

The type of sponsor you approach may determine exactly how you present your sponsorship proposal. Larger efforts may require a proposal that is very specific to your needs and the needs of that potential sponsor. Smaller businesses may simply choose their sponsorship from a menu of options you present on a standard solicitation form.

In both situations, your presentation needs to include the following information:

- Some information about your organization. Detail the scope of your program, how many sports it offers, how many athletes participate, and how many other students are involved.
- What is to be sponsored. You will need to detail your needs. If you develop a general proposal form, you can list some of the items that the sponsorship helps to support.
- What you can offer the sponsor. These are specific availabilities, a list generally reserved for the largest of sponsors.
- The benefits of being a sponsor. Sell the sponsor on the tangible and intangible benefits of being involved with your program.

Figure 8.1 (see pp. 123–125) is a sample sponsorship proposal to a large corporation and a general sponsorship rate card that may be circulated to smaller businesses. Each offers a variety of options, but the general rate card reads more like an *a la carte* menu of what may be individually purchased. If you're pitching a detailed proposal to a large company, you may be going for everything on the list.

Knowing Your Rights

A sponsor for a state high school championship, a family restaurant, was provided signage at the event site. Facility management approved the signage because it came from an event sponsor and was not permanent. However, there was one hitch. Another family restaurant chain owned the concession rights to the event site and displayed signage throughout.

When the corporate vice president (VP) of marketing for the restaurant chain responsible for the concessions at the arena sat down in his private box to view one of the contests, he saw six of his competitor's banners hanging on the wall surrounding the playing surface. He called building security and demanded the immediate removal of the signs. Security alerted state association personnel, who responded by recommending that the executive director of the building remind the VP about the event signage policy.

The incident did not affect the long-term relationship between the on-site restaurant and the venue. It is not unusual for signage contracts between venues and their corporate sponsors to include a clause which allows single-event signage even if the signage competes with that of the venue.

The sports director needs to be mindful of this situation when staging an event in an off-campus setting. Be sure to check with the site in these instances regarding its signage policy.

CONTACTING POTENTIAL SPONSORS

Once you have identified what you have to offer a corporate sponsor and who these potential sponsors are, the next step is approaching those parties. On the contact form (see Form 8.1, p. 120) is space for you to list the key sponsorship decision-makers at each business you wish to approach. Your contact could vary from business to business, depending on the size of the company and size of your community. If you live in a medium to small town where everyone knows everyone, your contacts are likely to be less formal.

Begin by determining whether the first contact with a potential sponsor should be by mail, telephone, or a personal meeting. If you have a parent or coach who has opened the door for you to make a proposal, use your best judgment to determine if that third party should be involved further in the contact process. Hopefully that individual has already sold the decision-maker on the benefits of sponsoring your program.

Cold calls, in which you are making a first call to a potential sponsor, should lay the groundwork for that sponsor to become interested in your program in general first, and later as a sponsor. These leads will take longer to cultivate than existing supporters. If contacting a company to obtain information about the appropriate contact, find out if a protocol exists for submitting sponsorship proposals. Many larger companies have recently established policies for evaluating unsolicited sponsorship proposals.

Follow that initial contact with a letter, requesting a brief meeting to discuss the possibility of a sponsorship (it is not necessary for a proposal to be a part of that correspondence, but you may wish to do so). Follow that letter with a phone call to confirm that your correspondence was received and to answer any initial questions. Then attempt to schedule an appointment. If you successfully schedule an appointment, make sure that the proposal you take to that meeting is tailored to that potential sponsor. You can do so easily by developing a standard proposal on your computer, then dropping in the name of the potential sponsor in specific locations.

Also ensure that your proposal is accompanied by samples of any printed materials you want the sponsor to help underwrite. Souvenir programs, schedule cards, and posters are items that should be presented and left with the potential sponsor for evaluation. If possible, send this information to the sponsor before your meeting.

The actual meeting may be an exploratory time for both parties. Discuss philosophies and goals, and be prepared for much give and take with larger companies. This is their way of finding out whether your proposal is truly everything you have to offer.

After your meeting, follow up with a thank-you letter, as well as a response to any questions you may not have been able to answer in the meeting. Sometimes a sponsor will request treatment for their involvement that you hadn't considered, and the thank-you letter gives you a chance to modify your proposal to address the sponsor's needs more directly. Don't be afraid to mention that you may call in a few days to see if they have any questions. Maintaining an active approach once the meeting is over is a good way to indicate your interest to the sponsor.

Don't be discouraged if a larger company takes a longer time than you prefer to make a decision or doesn't return phone calls. Unfortunately, many people in the marketing/advertising/sponsorship world are famous for not returning telephone calls.

Because the decision-making process in small businesses is generally less involved than in large businesses, the small business may only require a meeting over a cup of coffee and a verbal agreement about the terms of sponsorship. Small businesses often view their support of school sports as an essential element of their doing business in that community, and are generally enthusiastic about being involved.

DELIVERING ON YOUR PROMISES

Be sure to deliver whatever benefits you promise a sponsor. Document everything you do that recognizes the sponsor's name. Documentation includes, but is not limited to,

- copies of every printed piece that sponsor helps support (i.e., a program from every home athletic event in which the sponsor is mentioned),
- photographs indicating benefits like signage,
- any press releases that include the name of the sponsor (and if a newspaper prints the name of the sponsor connected to something happening at your school, be sure the sponsor receives a copy from you),
- copies of any public address announcer copy that acknowledges the sponsor at your events, and
- samples of any promotional giveaway items paid for by the sponsor.

If the sponsor made new uniforms possible for a team, sending that sponsor an autographed team picture (in the new uniforms) is an appropriate thank you and method of documentation.

Saved by the Clipping Service

A sports information director at a small college was in danger of having his position eliminated one year when the institution was going through a series of budget cuts. The publicist's position was unnecessary, the pencil pushers contended; what could it possibly do for the school?

At that point, the sports information director documented how much the position was worth to the college. Using file after file of newspaper clippings obtained from the school's clipping service, he not only illustrated the amount of publicity the position was generating for the teams there, but also how much it would cost if the school had to buy the newspaper space that was being generated by his press releases and postgame reporting. And, he pointed out, that was just in newspapers! It didn't take long for the school to save his position from the chopping block.

OBTAINING TITLE SPONSORSHIPS—PROS AND CONS

Most people have mixed feelings about title sponsorships of events. While it has become more and more accepted that the "New Castle Invitational" has become the "White Castle Hamburger Invitational," some feel that educational events should maintain the position that the school is the sponsor. Doing so helps the school maintain its own identity for that event and avoids the appearance of selling out to a corporation, where the event becomes one long commercial (similar to what's happened at some college and professional events).

One other down side to a title sponsorship is that the media are very reluctant to pick up the sponsor's banner and give the company free space in the newspaper. With nearly every college football game, and many other college and professional events, now bearing some kind of corporate name independent of or along with the traditional name, some newspaper style books now instruct writers to refer to an event by its full sponsored name in the first reference only. Subsequent references are to use the traditional name of the event. Some event sponsors have responded by demanding that a condition of their title sponsorship be that the traditional name be dropped entirely so that the media will have no alternative but to refer to the sponsor in each reference.

A title sponsor can be the difference between that event being staged and an open date appearing on your event calendar. But when considering the merits of a title sponsor, remember that some sponsors think giving you $200 worth of trophies makes them worthy of being a title sponsor. If you're going to sell the title of your event, make sure you get a lot more than trophies.

CONSIDER A LARGER EFFORT

One compelling reason to sell a large sponsorship package to a business is that it reduces the number of times you will contact that business for money. In chapter 4 we discussed combining athletic and nonathletic co-curricular programs in your public relations activities. With some advance planning, a unified approach to corporate sponsorships could reap large benefits for your school.

When money is involved, however, you will find that athletic and nonathletic groups may wish to contact completely different people—even within the same company. You may want to preserve individual relationships you have established for a particular activity.

MANAGING THE SPONSORSHIP SALES CALENDAR

When getting into corporate sponsorships, your sales approach should be like that of soliciting advertising—it should take place before the sports season or school year begins. The sponsorship selling process generally takes longer than the advertising sales process with large corporations. You will need a minimum of 3 months lead time to sell sponsorships. Even for smaller businesses, a change from what they have purchased in the past may require different budgeting. Once you have sold sponsorships, though, repeat sales fall into place because businesses which have had a positive experience plan on being called again.

We've mentioned before that businesses don't like to be continually hit on for support by different groups. If you can make one call take care of everything for an entire school year, it will be appreciated by sponsors. To that end, it makes sense to see if other groups within your organization may want to be involved in the sponsorship effort.

Coordinating the timing to involve other groups is a challenge. Just as big an obstacle is some natural competition that athletic and nonathletic groups competing for the community's support have felt for years. A unified effort may take a year to plan initially and may take the involvement of your administration at its highest levels. However, if the athletic program has involved a variety of other student groups, as is suggested throughout this book, a spirit of cooperation may have been fostered that will assist in making a unified sponsorship drive by sports, music, drama, and other clubs a viable option.

A Different Calendar

In the education world, you are accustomed to working on a school-year calendar, with the year usually beginning in July. When you sell corporate sponsorships, however, be alert to the business fiscal calendar and its effect.

A typical fiscal calendar in business coincides with the regular calendar. Some larger businesses may begin their involvement only in January, whereas others may be able to work with your school calendar.

If your cash-flow situation allows it, one option is to bill a corporate sponsor for its involvement in the latter part of one calendar year at the beginning of the next. This way, you can get a business working with your budget calendar. It can make the difference between being able to attract a sponsor and not having that company affiliated with your program.

EVALUATING YOUR SPONSORSHIP EFFORTS

Your contact sheets should maintain all activity taking place between you and your sponsors. Notes will also appear on actual event logs. It wouldn't hurt to list the sponsors on the forms we discussed previously to track each element of your promotion program (see Forms 3.1, 3.2, and 3.3 on pp. 24, 27, and 30 respectively). The evaluation form should list the size of the sponsorship the business purchased, when invoices were sent, when bills were paid, when documentation was sent; and the list goes on and on.

Summary

To obtain sponsorships for an effective promotion program,

1. recognize that each sponsor has a set of unique needs when it enters into a sponsorship. This is a business relationship, and the school needs to deliver on all the promises it makes to a business. Complete documentation is also a must;
2. tailor your sponsorship program so that different sponsors can underwrite the costs of different organizational needs;
3. use a variety of ways to identify potential sponsors, and vary your sales approach to each;
4. develop sponsorship proposals that contain information about the organization and its makeup. Although the needs in that particular sponsorship may also be presented, it is not uncommon to have a generic sponsorship package made up for presentation purposes;
5. follow certain procedures to make initial contact with a potential sponsor, and follow up as part of the process;
6. document what the sponsor receives in its sponsorship, including copies of souvenir programs and everything else in which the name appears;
7. consider title sponsorships, but remain conscious of drawbacks;
8. sell sponsorships well in advance of the coming school year, and include other clubs and groups within your school; and
9. consistently record everything you do with a sponsor to maintain that sponsor as a part of your program.

Form 8.1 Sponsorship Tracking

Sponsor Contact Log

Company

Contact: ______________________ Title: ______________________

Address: ______________________ Telephone: ______________________

______________________ Fax: ______________________

Met (referred by): ______________________

____

Key decision-makers: ______________________

____

Type of business: ______________________

____

Specific sport/event interests: ______________________

____

____

High school graduate/year: ______________________

High school athlete/sports/years/notes: ______________________

____

____

____

Family involvement with your school (brothers, sisters, children): ______________________

____

____

Other community interest/involvement/sponsorship: ______________________

____

____

Advertising resources (local, national, etc.): ______________________

____

Conversation Log

Time/date	Topic

Sponsorship Record

Date	Type of sponsorship	Cost

Notes: ____________________

____

____

Reaction/follow-up: ____________________

____

____

Date	Type of sponsorship	Cost

Notes: ____________________

____

____

Reaction/follow-up: ____________________

____

____

Montgomery High School
Sponsorship Proposal to Big Cat Company

Overview

Since 1925, Montgomery High School has played a pivotal role in helping to shape the lives of the young men and women of our community. Recognized nationally as a "school of distinction," Montgomery's academic programs are complemented by an 18-sport athletics program steeped in a tradition of excellence.

Montgomery High School is seeking a corporate partnership with Big Cat Company to help maintain that tradition in educational athletics, enriching both the lives of the youngsters that participate and the city of Montgomery.

Facts and Figures

- Of the 2,000 students in the high school, nearly 40% are participating in the interscholastic athletics program.
- Another 25% of the student body is associated with the athletics program through marching and pep bands, cheerleading and pom-pom squads, and various other support roles.
- Team members sport an academic grade point average of nearly a half-grade above that of the general student population.
- Athletic events in the 18 sports, all at the varsity, junior varsity, and freshman levels, total over 400 during a single school year, providing an additional learning environment for the participants.
- Home athletic events are attended by over 75,000 spectators every year, not only from this community, but from neighboring locales, who partake of various retail opportunities while visiting Montgomery, including restaurants and shopping centers.

The Proposal

Montgomery High School proposes that Big Cat Company become one of its four major corporate partners for the 199_–9_ school year. The following package is proposed:

Full media buy package. Includes sponsorship of radio broadcasts of all football, boys basketball, and girls basketball games; full-page, four-color ad on the back cover of the all-sports souvenir program produced for all home games in all sports; two-color ads on all-sports poster schedules and all-sports schedule cards produced each season. **Cost—$XX,000**

Sponsorship of gymnasium and athletic field scoreboards. Cost—$X,000

Major sponsorship of invitational tournament. Cost—$X,000

Sponsorship of Scholar-Athlete Award Program and banquet. Cost—$X,000

In addition, the following items will be provided:

- Big Cat Company will be recognized as an exclusive sponsor of Montgomery High School athletics.
- Twenty (20) all-sports family passes will be provided to the corporate office of Big Cat Company.
- Venue signage at major facilities in addition to scoreboard signage (where applicable).
- Message board time in gymnasium and athletic fields available.

(continued)

Figure 8.1 Sample sponsorship proposal and rate card.

- Full-page article on the Scholar-Athlete Award in souvenir programs, acknowledging the sponsorship of Big Cat Company.
- Mention in press releases.

Sponsorship Proposal Definitions

Sponsorship of all radio broadcasts. All of Montgomery High's varsity contests in football and boys and girls basketball will be broadcast on radio station KCAT in Montgomery. Big Cat Company would be mentioned as a sponsor during each broadcast, in addition to receiving six 30-second advertisements per game. A total of 50 contests, plus postseason tournament games, will be broadcast.

Full-page, four-color advertisement on back cover of all-sports souvenir programs. An all-sports program is produced each season and used at all home contests. Big Cat Company would be given the back cover position on those programs. Circulation for the school year is XX,000, and attendance at these events is over XX,000.

All-sports schedule posters and cards. Posters and pocket cards announcing the game schedules for all athletic teams are produced on a season basis. Big Cat Company would have a 6- x 20-inch panel across the bottom of the posters and the back panel of the cards. The ads on both would be two color. A quantity of X00 posters and X,000 schedule cards are produced each season and distributed throughout Montgomery.

Scoreboard sponsorship. Big Cat Company would receive one of the four large panels on the scoreboards in the school gymnasium; in the main stadium, where all football and soccer games are played; and on the baseball/softball fields. There are a total of XXX events at these facilities each school year, attracting XX,000 spectators.

Major sponsorship of invitational meet. Each school year, Montgomery High School stages multischool events in the following sports:

- Cross-country
- Golf
- Volleyball
- Soccer

As part of its sponsorship, Big Cat Company would help underwrite a major portion of the expenses incurred by Montgomery High for staging one of these events. Big Cat Company would be recognized as a title sponsor of the event.

Scholar-Athlete Award sponsorship. Big Cat Company would underwrite the costs of this program, recognizing the top three scholar-athletes on each team Montgomery sponsors at the varsity, junior varsity, and freshman levels. Each recipient would be recognized with a plaque, and a banquet for the recipients and their parents would be held at the end of the school year. School personnel would handle the selection of the award recipients.

Exclusive sponsor. With the media/signage buys and the Scholar-Athlete Award sponsorship, Montgomery High would recognize Big Cat Company as an exclusive sponsor and not allow a similar service to purchase a similar athletic sponsorship.

Family all-sports season tickets. The Big Cat Company would be given a set amount of family all-sports season tickets to Montgomery athletic events.

(continued)

Figure 8.1 *(continued)*

Venue signage. Big Cat Company, at its own expense, may provide banners to be hung at selected Montgomery home athletic events. Montgomery staff would be responsible for the placement of the banners.

Message board time. At selected events that have electronic message centers, Big Cat Company will be recognized as a corporate partner of Montgomery High School events.

Articles on the corporate partnership. Montgomery High School will provide Big Cat Company with editorial copy in its souvenir program series pertaining to the Scholar-Athlete Award sponsorship.

Mention in press releases. Montgomery High School will issue a press release, announcing the involvement of Big Cat Company in its year-round programs. In addition, Big Cat Company will be listed as the sponsor of the Scholar-Athlete Award in all releases pertaining to that program.

Montgomery High School
Individual Sponsorship Availabilities

Radio time	$X,000*
Multischool event expenses	X,000
Two-color, full-page ad all programs	X,000
Team banquet sponsorship	X00
Back-of-ticket advertisements	X00
Message board time (where available)	X00
Other souvenir program advertising	*See program rate card*
Schedule poster/card advertising	*See schedule rate card*
Tickets	Negotiable

*Four 30-second advertisements per game, plus opening and closing billboards

Figure 8.1 (*continued*)

Appendix A
Sample Signature Sheets

All with 50/50 editorial to advertising mix

16-page program

This program is printed in four-page signatures, using four signatures. You read the signatures from top to bottom, with the first signature being the pages closest to the front and back of the program, the fourth signature being the pages in the middle of the program. In this example, the copy for the pages on the fourth signature will change with each game, the topics will remain the same. The first, second, and third signatures are printed for the entire season.

First Signature

1 - Cover	2 - Ad
16 - Ad	15 - Ad

Second Signature

3 - Welcome letters (1/4 ad)	4 - Team photo/schedule (1/4 ad)
14 - Cheerleaders (1/2 ad)	13 - Freshman team photo (1/2 ad)

Third Signature

5 - Coaching staff photo (1/4 ad)	6 - 199_ Seniors and captains (1/4 ad)
12 - JV team photo (1/2 ad)	11 - School records (1/2 ad)

Fourth Signature

7 - Tonight's game preview (1/4 ad)	8 - Home rosters (1/4 ad)
10 - Feature story (1/4 ad)	9 - Visitor rosters (1/4 ad)

24-page program

This program is printed in three 8-page sections. The third section is printed game by game, the remainder of the season. Also note how the information which changes with each game, the underlined pages, is set up on one side of the sheet of the third signature.

First Signature

1 - Cover	2 - Ad
4 - Welcome letters (1/4 ad)	3 - Team photo/schedule (1/4 ad)

21 - Cheerleaders (1/2 ad)
22 - Freshman team photo (1/2 ad)
24 - Ad
23 - Ad

Second Signature

5 - Coaching staff photo (1/4 ad)
6 - 199_ Seniors and captains (1/4 ad)
8 - Individual photos (1/4 ad)
7 - Ad
17 - Fall team schedules (1/4 ad)
18 - Fall team schedules (1/4 ad)
20 - JV team photo (1/2 ad)
19 - School records (1/2 ad)

Third Signature

9 - Tonight's game preview (1/4 ad)
10 - Individual photos (1/4 ad)
12 - Home rosters (1/4 ad)
11 - Individual photos (1/2 ad)
13 - Visitor rosters (1/4 ad)
14 - Stadium information/records (1/4 ad)
16 - Feature story (1/4 ad)
15 - Ad

32-page program

This program is printed in four 8-page sections and is an all-sports program. The fourth section is printed game by game, the remainder for the season. Also note how the information which changes with each game, the underlined pages, is set up on one side of the sheet of the fourth signature.

First Signature

1 - Cover
2 - Ad
4 - Welcome letters (1/4 ad)
3 - Table of contents (1/2 ad)
29 - Marching band photo (1/4 ad)
30 - Varsity, JV, frosh cheerleaders pix
32 - Ad
31 - Ad

Second Signature

5 - Administration photo (1/2 ad)
6 - Group photo/coaching staffs (1/2 ad)
8 - Fall sports schedules (1/4 ad)
7 - Fall sports schedules (1/4 ad)
25 - Sportsmanship article (1/4 ad)
26 - Academic feature on Your H.S.
28 - Ad
27 - Ad

Third Signature

9 - Varsity football photo (1/2 ad)
10 - Varsity volleyball photo (1/2 ad)
12 - Ad
11 - Varsity boys soccer photo (1/2 ad)
21 - Ad
22 - Sub-varsity team photos (1/4 ad)
24 - Sub-varsity team photos (1/2 ad)
23 - Sub-varsity team photos (1/4 ad)

Fourth Signature

13 - Tonight's game preview (1/4 ad)
14 - Varsity swimming photo (1/2 ad)
16 - Home rosters (1/4 ad)
15 - Varsity golf photo (1/2 ad)
17 - Visitor rosters (1/4 ad)
18 - Varsity cross-country photos (1/4 ad)
20 - Feature story (1/4 ad)
19 - Varsity tennis photo (1/2 ad)

Appendix B
American Sport Education Program (ASEP) Leader Level Resources

Item	Item number	Unit price*
Leader Level Coaching Principles Course Materials		
Leader Level Coaching Principles Course (*Successful Coaching*, *Clinic Study Guide*, Course Processing, Diploma)	ACEP0080	30.00
Successful Coaching	PMAR0376	18.00
Coaching Principles Instructor Guide (Rev. 3rd Ed.)	ACEP0007	70.00
Coaching Principles Clinic Study Guide (package of 10)	ACEP0033	22.50
Coaching Principles Leadership Training Seminar	ACEP0056	299.00
Leader Level Coaching Principles Videotape Set (5)	MACE0100	325.00
Coaching Philosophy Videotape	MACE0101	70.00
Sport Psychology Videotape	MACE0102	70.00
Sport Pedagogy Videotape	MACE0103	70.00
Sport Physiology Videotape	MACE0104	70.00
Sport Management Videotape	MACE0105	70.00
NFICEP Coaching Principles Course Materials		
NFICEP Coaching Principles Course (*Successful Coaching*, *Clinic Study Guide*, Course Processing, Diploma)	ACEP0083	30.00
Successful Coaching (NFICEP Edition)	ACEP0064	18.00
Coaching Principles Instructor Guide	ACEP0005	70.00
Coaching Principles Leadership Training Seminar	ACEP0058	299.00

NFICEP Coaching Principles Videotape Set (5)	MNFI0100	325.00
Coaching Philosophy Videotape	MNFI0101	70.00
Sport Psychology Videotape	MNFI0102	70.00
Sport Pedagogy Videotape	MNFI0103	70.00
Sport Physiology Videotape	MNFI0104	70.00
Sport Management Videotape	MNFI0105	70.00
Leader Level Sport First Aid Course Materials		
Leader Level Sport First Aid Course (*Sport First Aid*, *Clinic Study Guide*, Course Processing, Diploma)	ACEP0081	30.00
Sport First Aid	PFLE0410	18.00
Sport First Aid Instructor Guide	ACEP0004	70.00
Sport First Aid Clinic Study Guide (package of 10)	ACEP0036	22.50
Sport First Aid Leadership Training Seminar	ACEP0068	199.00
Leader Level Sport First Aid Videotape	MACE0106	125.00
NFICEP Sport First Aid Course Materials		
NFICEP Sport First Aid Course (*Sport First Aid*, *Clinic Study Guide*, Course Processing, Diploma)	ACEP0082	30.00
Sport First Aid (NFICEP Edition)	ACEP0065	18.00
Sport First Aid Instructor Guide	ACEP0006	70.00
Sport First Aid Leadership Training Seminar	ACEP0070	199.00
Leader Level Sport First Aid Videotape	MNFI0106	125.00
Leader Level/NFICEP Drugs and Sport Course Materials		
Coaches Guide to Drugs and Sport	PRIN0715	17.95
Leader Level Sport Techniques and Tactics Resources		
Coaching Basketball Successfully	PWOO0446	18.95
Coaching Girls' Basketball Successfully	PHUT0343	20.00
Coaching Football Successfully	PREA0518	18.95
Coaching Swimming Successfully	PHAN0492	18.95
Coaching Tennis Successfully	PUST0461	18.95
Coaching Volleyball Successfully	PNEV0362	18.00
Leader Level SportDirector Resources		
Event Management for SportDirectors	ACEP0320	20.00
Program Evaluation for SportDirectors	PKES0505	20.00
Promotion for SportDirectors	PJOH0722	20.00

Glossary

carnival events—A form of in-game promotion, usually conducted during breaks in the action (e.g., time-outs, intermissions, halftimes), such as halfcourt basketball shots and hockey Score-O. These promotions often are linked to a large giveaway item because a participant's chance of success is so unlikely.

corporate sponsor—A business providing revenues to your sports program for daily funding or add-ons in exchange for exposure considerations.

cross promotions—Combining several individual events and promotions to create a single, large event.

general giveaways—A series of general, inexpensive products (e.g., miniature balls, pompoms, bells, kazoos, towels, and sunglasses) underwritten by a sponsor and imprinted with the sponsor's logo and given away periodically throughout the year.

in-game promotions—Promotions conducted during a contest to enhance your local product and promote school spirit, such as giveaways and intermission activities.

mass media—Electronic forms of communication including radio, television, cable, computer, and still newer opportunities.

media relations—Delivering your message to print and electronic or broadcast representatives and accommodating the needs of the media personnel covering your program.

media specialist—A person having regular dialog (e.g., calls about postgame results, providing information, serving as a host at your events) with media representatives about your school.

pregame promotions—Promotions conducted to draw attention to and sell tickets for an upcoming event.

press box/row—A working area for game administration and media assigned to report on a contest at your school. Not a haven for non-workers or a skybox for school administrators or booster club members.

print promotions—Using various printed materials, such as schedule cards and game programs, to promote your program posters.

public relations—Interacting with various groups within your organization and the public community to deliver your message.

public service announcement (PSA)—Airtime provided by a radio or television station to nonprofit organizations to help them promote their causes. PSAs are aired as traditional-sounding commercials or during community calendar or bulletin board programs.

publicity—Efforts within your control to promote your school; usually free opportunities, with the only investment being your time and energy.

rate card—A price list of advertising opportunities your organization can provide to a potential advertiser. Called a card originally because of the thickness of the paper stock it was printed on.

rights fee—Monetary charges that a radio, television, or cable outlet pays to a school, game organizer, or tournament sponsor for the opportunity to broadcast a game. Rights are owned by the home school for games during the season and by the tournament sponsor for postseason contests.

signage—Signs displayed at your athletic events, usually recognizing the contribution of a corporate sponsor.

signature—A 4-, 8-, or 16-page section of a game program or other publication.

speaker's bureau—A service you offer to provide coaches, administrators, and student-athletes to groups looking for speakers (and an opportunity to get your message out to the public in a positive forum).

specific giveaways—A form of cross promotion linked to a specific item, such as a marked program or seat. These giveaways are conducted on a regular schedule.

title sponsorship—Selling the name of an event to a corporate sponsor, usually at a premium price. For example, the Bronco Invitational might become the King's Castle Hamburger Invitational.

trade advertising—Trading advertising space or other promotional considerations with a business in return for services or products given to your program.

Index

Page numbers in bold refer to forms.

About the Author

John R. Johnson, communications director of the Michigan High School Athletic Association (MHSAA), has worked in sports promotion and publicity for more than 20 years. He first became interested in promotion as a high school student responsible for reporting the results of his school's sports teams to the media. His interest grew during college when he assisted in the sports information department at Michigan State University (MSU) and subsequently as the sports information director at Albion (Michigan) College.

After earning a BA in Journalism in 1979, John began working full-time in sports promotion, first in the sports information department at Western Michigan University, then at Indiana University. In 1987, John became the first communications director of the MHSAA, working to promote and publicize the athletic programs of more than 1,300 senior high, junior high, and middle schools.

John has assisted with the coordination of media for the 1984 men's Olympic basketball trials, directed press operations for a number of college and high school championship events, and developed a model sportsmanship public relations campaign for schools in Michigan. He has won numerous awards for the many quality publications he produced while working in college sports information.

American Sport Education Program

Leader Level

ASEP's Leader Level provides quality resources and courses for coaches and administrators in interscholastic and club sport. In fact, the National Federation of State High School Associations has selected the Leader Level SportCoach Courses as its own coaches education program, called NFICEP–National Federation Interscholastic Coaches Education Program. The Leader Level offers the following:

Leadership Training Seminars

Our Leadership Training Seminars (LTSs) not only show sport administrators how to conduct our courses, they also revitalize them with fresh ideas about how to help coaches be more effective in their coaching roles. Leader Level instructor seminars include the

- Coaching Principles Seminar,
- Sport First Aid Seminar, and
- Drugs and Sport Seminar (in development).

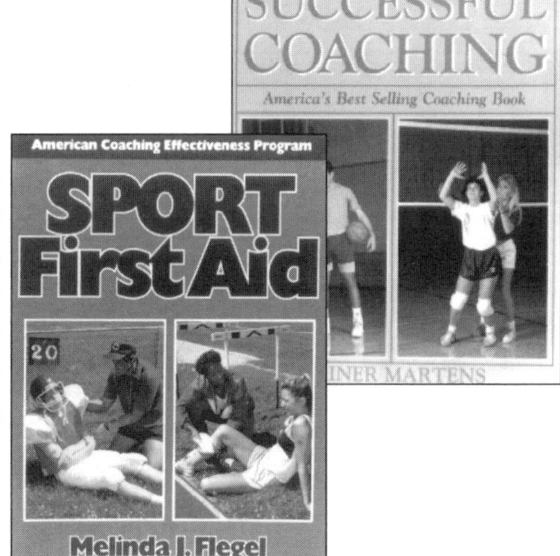

Coaches Courses

Once administrators have attended our LTSs, they are prepared to teach our **Coaching Principles Course** and **Sport First Aid Course,** and soon, the **Drugs and Sport Course** to coaches. The courses provide excellent educational opportunities for both new and experienced coaches. At each course, coaches attend a clinic, study the course text and study guide, then take an open-book test.

The Coaching Successfully Series

The books in this series explain how to teach fundamental sports skills and strategies as well as how to build a sports program by applying principles of philosophy, psychology, and teaching and management methods to coaching.

Series Titles

- Coaching Tennis Successfully
- Coaching Swimming Successfully
- Coaching Football Successfully
- Coaching Basketball Successfully
- Coaching Volleyball Successfully
- Coaching Girls' Basketball Successfully
- Coaching Baseball Successfully

SportDirector Series

See facing page for information.

For more information about ASEP and the Leader Level, call toll-free 1-800-747-5698.

Other Resources in the SportDirector Series

Program Evaluation for SportDirectors

James L. Kestner

1996 • Paper • Approx 120 pp • Item PKES0505
ISBN 0-87322-505-X • $20.00 ($29.95 Canadian)

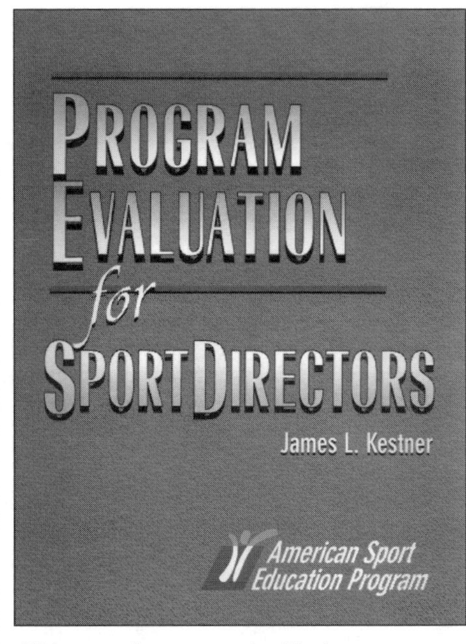

Program Evaluation for SportDirectors is a practical, hands-on resource that you can use to evaluate your personnel, facilities and equipment, and program offerings. It contains an easy-to-follow blueprint for conducting evaluations and 20 field-tested forms that can be used or modified to fit your specific evaluation needs.

First, you'll learn how to prepare for an effective program evaluation. The book explains how to reflect on personal and organizational philosophies, identify who will help in the evaluation process, assess which programs and individuals need to be evaluated, develop an evaluation plan, implement the plan, and review and revise the plan.

The heart of the book shows you how to conduct the actual evaluations. You'll learn to conduct personnel evaluations and discover new methods for evaluating facilities, equipment, and athletic programs.

Event Management for SportDirectors

American Sport Education Program

1996 • Spiral • 144 pp • Item ACEP0320
ISBN 0-87322-968-1 • $20.00 ($29.95 Canadian)

Event Management for SportDirectors is a handy tool for planning and managing practically any type or size of athletic event. The book provides a comprehensive checklist of 18 categories (with tasks to be completed for each category), allowing you to conduct even the most complicated functions in a systematic and organized manner.

This time-saving resource shows you how to plan and manage the following areas of an event:

- Event objectives
- Finances
- Rules and officials
- Coach development
- Risk management
- Registration
- Communications
- Event evaluation
- Awards
- Food service
- Transportation
- Housing
- Promotion
- Public relations
- Facility needs
- Staffing
- Practice and competition schedules
- Equipment, uniforms, and supplies

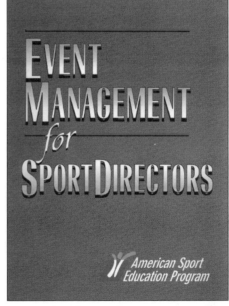

To place your order, U.S. customers **call TOLL FREE 1 800 747-4457**. Customers outside the U.S. place your order using the appropriate telephone number/address shown in the front of this book.

Prices are subject to change.

Human Kinetics
The Premier Publisher for Sports & Fitness

2335

Chinese Art III